SPORTS SCIENCE

# THE SCIENCE OF GYMNASTICS

AMY B. ROGERS



ROSEN PUBLISHING

Published in 2026 by The Rosen Publishing Group, Inc.
2544 Clinton Street, Buffalo, NY 14224



Portions of this work were originally authored by Heather E. Schwartz and published as *Gymnastics*. All new material this edition authored by Amy B. Rogers.



Designer: Rachel Rising
Editor: Jill Keppeler

Cataloging-in-Publication Data

Names: Rogers, Amy B.
Title: The science of gymnastics / Amy B. Rogers.
Description: Buffalo, NY : Rosen Publishing, 2026. | Series: Sports science | Includes glossary and index.
Identifiers: ISBN 9781499479423 (pbk.) | ISBN 9781499479430 (library bound) | ISBN 9781499479447 (ebook)
Subjects: LCSH: Gymnastics--Juvenile literature. | Sports sciences--Juvenile literature.
Classification: LCC GV461.3 R64 2026 | DDC 796.44--dc23



*Manufactured in the United States of America*

CPSIA Compliance Information: Batch #CSRYA26. For further information, contact Rosen Publishing at 1-800-237-9932.

# CONTENTS

# FOREWORD

The way that high-caliber athletes perform can seem unbelievable. To many people watching in the stands or from home, their feats may seem unreal—as unlikely as learning to fly. Even regular players and participants in these sports may stare in awe, feeling like they can never reach those heights.

However, the laws of nature are still the law and still unbreakable, and once you learn more about how the science behind these sports works, they're in some ways even more amazing. Peak athletes use the laws of nature and science to achieve their unbelievable feats, and understanding these laws can give you an even greater appreciation for their achievements. Science makes the incredible understandable and the seemingly unreal real. Rather than ruining an appreciation for sports, it can deepen our understanding and increase our awe.

In these books, readers can learn more about the scientific ideas behind athletic achievements, from the simplest hit in baseball to the most amazing gymnastics flip. Physics principles such as gravity, friction and drag, and Newton's laws of motion can all be applied to sports—and this means all sports, including swimming, football, track, and lacrosse. Readers will also learn about other scientific aspects of sports, including the whys and hows of athletic training, the principles of sports medicine, and the advances in technology that will affect these fields for years to come. This understanding can help young athletes better train for their sport, avoid injury, and better care for injuries when they happen.

These principles and ideas are presented in clear, understandable ways, with relatable and clear examples, including quotes from those who play and participate in the sports, those who coach and help them, and those who study the science behind it all.

While science may seem unrelatable, this set will give readers a reason (or many reasons) to question that assessment. Science is real, and it affects every aspect of our lives, even the things we do and watch for the sheer fun of it.

Sports and science are intrinsically intertwined. The basic principles of sports are the basic laws of science, and understanding one side will help you understand the other better. This is true for sports fans and young scientists alike!

Gymnasts, like all athletes, accomplish amazing feats that can be explained by science!

# CHAPTER ONE

# ART AND SCIENCE

Of all the various sports at the Summer Olympics, gymnastics may be the most popular. Viewers eagerly await the events, watching to see what (seemingly) physics-defying moves the sport's stars will undertake this time. The sport first developed as a collection of exercises in ancient Greece, but it has grown and changed over time to captivate today's sports fans with its mix of artistic expression and sheer athleticism. As Chloe Angyai of the *Huffington Post* wrote:

> *There are few things more thrilling than watching a gymnast launch herself into a tumbling series on the ... balance beam, or watching her whip her body around the high bar into a dazzling dismount followed by an improbable rock-solid stuck landing. Gymnastics, as gymnasts and coaches know, is physics; it's governed by the rules of inertia, momentum, and rotation, like the rest of the world. To outside viewers, though, it can seem more magic than physics—how else to explain how these young women manipulate their bodies into feats that ought to be physically impossible? No wonder it's a must-watch on NBC every four years.*[1]

Gymnasts excel at making the seemingly impossible look effortless. These athletes perform amazing feats of strength, flexibility, balance, and agility. Judges award points based on their execution of these skills. It takes years of training, proper nutrition, and plenty of natural ability to become an elite gymnast, and it also takes a strong understanding of science.

Shown here is Simone Biles, who is often considered the greatest gymnast of all time. Her skills seem to defy gravity, but they are actually examples of physics!

By understanding the science behind the sport, gymnasts can become better at its many aspects, coaches can help them achieve their best, and fans can develop a deeper appreciation for what these talented athletes can do. Each event in gymnastics is an example of science in action. This has been true from the sport's earliest days.

## BIOMECHANICS

Some gymnastics skills seem to defy the laws of science as the athetes push their body beyond its limits. In reality, however, these skills work within biomechanical principles. Biomechanics is the science of how the body moves. It also refers to the effects of natural forces, such as gravity, on the body.

**TWIST AND TURN** The types of gymnastics seen in Olympic competition are artistic gymnastics, rhythmic gymnastics, and trampoline.

Although gymnasts may be born with some genetic advantages or natural talents, they also train their bodies to stretch muscles and ligaments and improve flexibility. This training allows gymnasts to perform difficult tricks, especially tricks that involve flipping and twisting in the air.

When gymnasts launch into the air, they may appear to overcome scientific forces. As Reeves Wiedeman wrote in the *New Yorker* about Olympic champion Simone Biles, "Seeing Biles next to her competition … I felt as if [famous scientist] Isaac Newton had written a different set of laws on her behalf."[2] However, gymnasts are actually adhering to those laws. While performing a vault, for example, gymnasts do not disprove the existence of gravity. Instead, they demonstrate an idea developed by Newton, a mathematician and physicist of the late 17th and early 18th centuries. Newton developed three laws of motion. His first law says an object in motion tends to stay in motion unless acted on by another force. The same is true for an object at rest; it stays at rest without an outside force acting on it. Newton's second law says the acceleration of an object is related to the force acting upon it. Newton's third law says for every action, there is an equal and opposite reaction. During a vault, gymnasts run and jump hard onto a springboard in front of the apparatus (which is called a vault or vaulting table). The force downward on the springboard creates an equal force upward—an example of Newton's third law. This opposite reaction helps gymnasts gain height in the air despite the force of gravity pulling them down.

## EARLY ORIGINS

Many aspects of gymnastics have changed a lot over the sport's long history. The skills practiced and displayed by the earliest gymnasts were far from the high-flying feats seen in Olympic competition and other events today. However, the focus on demonstrating physical skill and mental focus through a series of exercises has remained the same. Even the clothing ancient gymnasts wore—or did not wear—made them look very different from today's athletes. The word "gymnastics" comes from the Greek word that means "to exercise naked," and it originally referred to a set of fitness activities that took place in the gymnasiums of ancient Greece, which the male athletes performed without any clothes.

Physical fitness was prized in ancient Greek culture. Back then, people practiced gymnastics by doing activities such as running, jumping, swimming, wrestling, boxing, and lifting

Shown here are German gymnasts who competed in the 1896 Olympic Games. Unlike the ancient Greeks, these gymnasts wore clothes!

weights. These sports, which are now considered their own areas of athletics, were originally grouped together under the broad label of "gymnastics" in the ancient world.

Practicing gymnastic exercises, such as wrestling and boxing, prepared Greek citizens for battle. Gymnastics practice also got competitors ready for the Olympic Games, which originated in Greece in celebration of the god Zeus. The first recorded Olympic Games were held in 776 BCE, and they continued every four years until about 393 CE.

Although women practiced gymnastics, only men were allowed in early Olympic competitions. Athletes had to compete naked. Some experts believe this was to keep the competitions safe, since there was no clothing to trip over. Others say the ancient Greeks simply accepted nudity and celebrated the male body in this way. Nudity may also have been required so that male athletes could show off their fitness and form in gymnastic events, which did not look like modern gymnastic events. Instead, ancient Olympic gymnastic competitions involved what we consider today to be track and field events, wrestling, and other examples of physical fitness.

After Rome conquered Greece, the Romans took up gymnastics themselves. They used the sport mainly as military training and not for athletic competition. The Olympic Games were eventually abolished by the Roman emperor Theodosius I. As a Christian, he did not support their pagan origins. Without the Olympic Games, interest in gymnastics as a sport faded. Centuries passed before it evolved into the modern sport known today. However, the concept of tumbling, which continues to be an important part of gymnastics, was kept alive by the Chinese and later, by groups of traveling performers in Europe during the Middle Ages.

## ROOTS OF THE MODERN SPORT

It wasn't until the late 18th century that modern gymnastics got its start. In 1793, a German teacher named Johann Christoph Friedrich Guts Muths published the book *Gymnastics for Youth*, detailing a program to improve balance, flexibility, and strength. That program formed the foundation for what we know today as the sport of gymnastics.

Physical education teachers all over the world read Guts Muths's book and put it into practice with their students. Over hundreds of years, generations of teachers and students developed and evolved the sport according to different beliefs about what constituted gymnastics and the best reasons to practice the sport. According to Guts Muths, gymnastics could be practiced for physical health and for artistic expression, and those who studied his teachings typically focused on one aspect or the other.

Friedrich Ludwig Jahn, another German educator, was one of Guts Muths's readers. In 1811, he opened a gymnasium near Berlin, Germany, where he focused his training on building students' muscular strength. He developed special new equipment for his students to use, including a high bar, parallel bars, and rings. In addition, he developed an early balance beam. Today, he is known as the father of modern gymnastics.

Franz Nachtegall, who was from Denmark, also read Guts Muths's book and went on to use gymnastics in the training of the Danish military. One of his students, Per Henrik Ling, who was from Sweden, developed the sport further by focusing on specific movements, body positions, and exercises, known as calisthenics. Ling's free calisthenics, which are exercises that do not require the use of anything but the body, would eventually become the gymnastic event known as the floor exercise.

## THE OLYMPICS RETURN

Gymnastics grew in popularity and reach. In 1881, representatives from gymnastics associations in Belgium, France, and the Netherlands met to form what is now called the Fédération Internationale de Gymnastique (FIG), which is also known as the International Gymnastics Federation. The creation of an international governing organization made it easier for international gymnastic competitions to take place.

Fifteen years after the FIG was created, gymnastics became a modern Olympic sport. The first modern Olympic Games

Shown here is an example of rhythmic gymnastics in action.

were held in 1896 in Athens, Greece. Competitors came from different countries to participate in the events, including rope climbing and vaulting. In the early years, only male gymnasts were allowed to compete. Female gymnasts began competing in 1928.

Until 1984, artistic gymnastics was the only discipline represented at the Olympic Games. Modern artistic gymnastics incorporates several different events. Male gymnasts perform on the pommel horse, which is an apparatus made of a padded metal frame set on a stand, and the rings, which hang from cables attached to a frame. Female gymnasts perform on the balance beam, which is a 3.9-inch (10 cm) wide beam that stands 4 feet (1.2 m) high. All gymnasts perform on bars. Men compete on the parallel bars and horizontal bar, while women compete on the uneven bars. The gymnasts grip the bars and swing around them to perform tricks. Floor exercise and vault events exist for both male and female gymnasts. Floor routines include tumbling and acrobatic tricks. In the vault event, gymnasts launch themselves over the vault using a springboard, flipping in the air before they land.

In 1984, rhythmic gymnastics was added to Olympic competition. This branch of gymnastics, which is practiced only by women at the Olympics, involves routines set to music. These routines often look like dances. Rhythmic gymnasts are also known for their use of objects—known as hand apparatuses—such as ropes, hoops, balls, clubs, and ribbons. Rhythmic gymnasts use muscle strength to point their toes, keep their legs straight and tight, and control their form so each move is precisely executed. They demonstrate flexibility with splits and kicks that extend their legs 180 degrees or more. In order to earn the highest points, their performance also needs unique choreography. Their jumps, pivots, leaps, balance, and flexibility are all evaluated for their final score.

In 2000, Olympic gymnastics expanded once again to include trampoline as an event for men and women. Competitors perform a routine in which they touch the trampoline a certain number of times and use the height it gives them to execute a variety of tricks that they are scored on. Gymnasts performing on the trampoline are judged on their form in three positions. In a tuck, the knees are bent and the hands touch the legs below the knees. In a pike position, gymnasts' legs must be straight and angled less than 135 degrees from the hip. Their hands should touch the tops of their feet in this position. In a straight position, gymnasts' legs must also be straight, angled more than 135 degrees from the hip.

## RISE OF THE STARS

For a long stretch in the 1900s, Eastern Europe was the center of the gymnastics world. During this span, countries such as the Soviet Union—which later divided into Russia and other smaller nations—produced gymnasts who won most of the Olympic medals in the sport.

By the 1960s, Romania was gearing up to challenge the countries dominating gymnastics at the time. A Romanian physical education teacher named Bela Karolyi started teaching gymnastics to girls in his country. At seven to eleven years old, his students were much younger than most competitive gymnasts at the time. Karolyi's young students spent much more time practicing than other gymnasts. They won local and regional competitions and performed well in national competitions, gaining the government's attention. Soon, Karolyi was asked to join a national effort to train Romania's first generation of gymnasts to compete at an international level. Karolyi had one goal in mind as a gymnastics coach: He wanted to beat the gymnasts from the Soviet Union, including the country's star gymnast at time, Olga Korbut. Karolyi found the gymnast who would help him do exactly that when he began training a young girl named Nadia Comăneci.

At the 1976 Olympic Games in the Canadian city of Montreal, Comăneci was only 14 years old when she became the first gymnast in Olympic history to score a perfect 10. Under the system of scoring at that time, Comăneci performed routines that were worth a maximum of 10 points. If she had made mistakes, points would have been deducted. Instead, she earned seven perfect 10 scores during that competition. She also earned three gold medals, including the all-around gold medal, which is awarded to the best overall gymnast in the competition.

Comăneci has said that, like most things in gymnastics, scoring a perfect 10 was the result of training and hard work rather than magic: "I did what I used to do every day in the gym. It's not like overnight I'd done something to surprise myself … It was a magic day, but it wasn't a magic day because I did something I didn't know I was going to do. I'd done those things in training."[3]

## A NAMESAKE MOVE

The greatest modern gymnasts do not just perform difficult skills, they also invent new ones. Nadia Comăneci demonstrated skills

Nadia Comăneci, shown here, was barely a teenager when she changed the sport of gymnastics forever by achieving a perfect score at the Olympics.

that had never been performed before in competition. When that happens, those moves are often named after the gymnast who first executed them. One famous move named after Nadia Comăneci is the Comăneci salto. It is performed on the uneven bars. To execute this move, the gymnast swings away from a support position on the high bar, and then she releases her hands to do a straddled front flip in the air before grabbing the high bar again.

"I always wanted to do the impossible, so when Bela [Karolyi] came up with the idea for the Comaneci salto, I was eager to try to perfect the skill," Comăneci wrote in her book *Letters to a Young Gymnast*. "A similar move was already being performed from the low bar to the high bar. Bela thought I could do it all on the high bar by catching the same bar I'd released. I spent

## EVEN THE SCOREBOARD WAS STUNNED

When Nadia Comăneci earned her first perfect score at the 1976 Olympics for her uneven bars routine, she did not immediately know she had achieved perfection. This was because the scoreboard did not actually reflect her score. It read "1.00" instead of "10" because the scoreboards at the time were only able to go up to 9.99, which until then, had been the highest score someone could achieve in Olympic competition. Because of this glitch, Comăneci initially believed she had received a one-point deduction on her routine instead of a perfect score.

Comăneci has said that the inability for even the scoreboard to process her achievement helped it become a legendary moment in the sport: "If the scoreboard would have been OK to show the 10, would the impact have been the same? Even an electronic thing was not able to show that … It probably made the story a little bigger."[1] Even the most advanced technology on the sport's biggest stage could not keep up with her achievements.

1. Quoted in Nancy Armour, "40 Years After Perfect 10, Gymnast Nadia Comăneci Remains an OlympicIcon," *USA Today*, July 20, 2016. www.usatoday.com/story/sports/olympics/rio-2016/2016/07/20/10-gymnast-nadia-comaneci-olympics-montreal/87357146/.

countless hours, days, weeks, and months perfecting the never before attempted skill."[4]

Russian gymnast Olga Korbut, who dominated the 1972 Olympics, invented the Korbut salto, which is a backward aerial somersault performed on the balance beam, and the Korbut flip, which is a backflip performed on the uneven bars. Japanese gymnast Mitsuo Tsukahara, a star at the 1968, 1972, and 1976 Olympic Games, invented the Tsukahara vault. He jumped off the springboard and did a half twist before pushing off the vaulting table backward.

In 1983, Natalia Yurchenko, a Russian gymnast, introduced a difficult new vault. To perform the move, Yurchenko ran toward the vault, then did a round-off to land facing backward on the springboard. She launched off the springboard, and as she went over the vault, she touched it with her hands. Pushing off from

Simone Biles, shown here, has multiple moves named after her in different events.

this back-handspring takeoff, she performed a twist in the air before landing.

The move required speed and especially control, because it was riskier than other moves on the vault. Landing backward on the springboard meant Yurchenko could not see the vault. She risked misplacing her hands and hitting her head at a high speed.

The rush to beat the competition was on. "The Yurchenko" became a standard move that gymnasts incorporated into their routines. However, it was still considered a dangerous move that landed many aspiring Olympians in the hospital. In 1989, American gymnast Kelly Garrison described her struggles with the Yurchenko to the *Los Angeles Times*: "I crashed probably

**TWIST AND TURN** Today, Yurchenko vaults are the most common type of vaults in gymnastics.

about 30 or 40 times (in training)," she said. "I had a lot of bruises, but nothing serious. I'm very fortunate, as many times as I landed on my head."[5]

One of the most famous "signature moves" in recent gymnastics history is "the Biles," which was named after Simone Biles and was introduced in Olympic competition at the 2016 Olympic Games in Rio de Janeiro, Brazil. This move, performed during the floor exercise, involves the gymnast doing two full backward flips in a layout position, with her body straight. At the end of the second flip, the gymnast turns her body 180 degrees to land facing forward. This kind of landing is very difficult because the gymnast cannot see the ground as she approaches the landing. This is why it is sometimes called a blind landing. It's very important for a gymnast to have a good sense of where they are in the air.

## AGE REQUIREMENTS

The rules for competing in gymnastics have changed over the years, just as the skills involved have evolved. When Karolyi began churning out young champions, female gymnasts in their 20s and 30s had no chance against them. The new top gymnasts, who had not yet reached puberty, were smaller and more flexible, which made it easier for them to do tricks.

Some began to fear that gymnastics was developing into a sport in which only children could compete on the elite level. Organizations then enacted rules that set minimum ages for gymnasts competing in the Olympics.

Before 1981, the minimum age for female gymnastics competitors in the Olympic Games was 14. That year, the age requirement was raised to 15. In 1997, the minimum age was raised again to 16 for all gymnasts.

During the 2008 Olympic Games in Beijing, China, controversy erupted over the age of one gymnast. The news media reported Chinese gymnast He Kexin's age as 13, which led to questions about the ages of other gymnasts on her team. Some people thought the Chinese gymnasts were exceptionally small and looked too young to be 16-year-old young women.

After the Chinese women's team won two gold medals and two bronze medals, the FIG determined the gymnasts' documents proved they were old enough to compete. Still, the controversy raised questions about cheating and highlighted the fact that gymnastics was still a sport where youth could

Oksana Chusovitina, right, has proven that gymnasts can still succeed even in their 40s!

**TWIST AND TURN** As of 2025, the United States has not won any medals in either Olympic rhythmic or trampoline gymnastics.

give athletes an edge, both physically and mentally. As John Geddert, the head coach of the 2012 U.S. women's Olympic gymnastics team once said, "Without sounding condescending to young women, this is a little girl's sport … With their body changes and the wear-and-tear everybody goes through, once they become women, it just becomes very, very difficult."[6]

Modern female gymnasts are proving Geddert wrong, however. Both Gabby Douglas and Aly Raisman competed for the United States in both the 2012 and 2016 Olympics, a feat that was once rarely accomplished in women's gymnastics. In 2016, Raisman won the silver medal in the all-around competition, which was a better showing than she had in 2012, showing that she improved with age. Raisman stated as much herself in 2016: "I feel like I'm better than I [was] in 2012, so I'm very proud of that."[7]

Another competitor in the 2016 Olympic Games who aimed to prove that gymnastics was not just a "little girl's sport" was Oksana Chusovitina of Uzbekistan. Chusovitina was 41 years old when she competed in Rio, which made her the oldest female gymnast in Olympic history, and, according to the *New York Times*, she did not seem ready to slow down any time soon:

> *"It's not very difficult," Chusovitina said, adding that she can't explain the reasons for her longevity in the sport. "This is a kind of experiment. I would like to see how long I can compete."*
>
> *Does that mean she will be back for the 2020 Games, in Tokyo, at 45?*
>
> *She smiled as she said, "Of course."*[8]

Chusovitina backed that statement up too. When competing at the 2020 Summer Olympics (which took place in 2021 because of the COVID-19 pandemic), Chusovitina was 46 years old.

Another gymnast proving that age might not be as much of a factor as previously thought is Simone Biles. She has competed in three Olympic Games to date, winning the all-around title in 2016 and again in 2024.

## SCORING CHANGES

Other numerical matters associated with gymnastics have also changed over time. The sport's scoring system has changed too. There is no more perfect 10 as there was in the days of

Simone Biles is shown here on the far left at the 2016 Olympics. This was her first Olympic appearance, but it was far from her last.

Nadia Comăneci. Gymnasts now receive two scores: one for the difficulty of their routine and the other for their execution of skills. The first score begins at 0, and points are added based on the skills they demonstrate; the second score begins at 10.0, and points are taken away, or deducted, for mistakes. The scores are then combined; a high score is typically in the range of 16 to 17 or slightly higher.

The new scoring was put in place after a scoring controversy at the 2004 Olympic Games in Athens, Greece. It was introduced in 2005 and made its Olympic debut in 2008, but not everyone in the gymnastics community has been happy about the change. Under the new system, gymnasts no longer had the potential to earn a perfect 10. Also, many were quick to point out that no matter how many times the scoring system is tweaked, it will still have flaws. "It's still not a perfect system," Martha Karolyi, the U.S. women's national team coordinator at the time, said in 2008. "It's still judges deciding to give a credit to a skill or not. It's still going to have errors because human beings are making the decisions."[9] However, the new scoring system did become less subjective than the old system.

## GROWING AND CHANGING

Over time, the United States began to establish itself as a force to be reckoned with in the world of gymnastics, especially women's gymnastics. In 1996, the Olympic Games in Atlanta, Georgia, marked the first time an American team won women's gymnastics gold. That team, known as the Magnificent Seven, inspired later teams such as 2012's Fierce Five, 2016's Final Five, and 2024's Golden Girls. In 2021, the U.S. women's team won silver, but it returned to gold again at the 2024 Olympics.

In 2016, it was said that the U.S. team set "a new standard in gymnastics,"[10] but it is certain that the standard will continue to change as the athletes and the sport itself change. Gymnastics will continue to evolve. New skills, new training methods, new technological advances, and their own dedication push each generation of gymnasts far beyond what their predecessors could do.

CHAPTER TWO

# BALANCE BASICS

The routines the Olympic gymnasts perform are incredible demonstrations of art and science, but long before they reach that point, they have to learn and master the basics of the sport. These skills become the foundation that gymnasts build on to grow in their sport. Although moves such as somersaults and splits might appear simple compared to what Olympic-level gymnasts can do, they are not easy to master. Even simpler skills require balance, flexibility, and strength.

Basic gymnastics skills can be a great way to see science in action. Each movement—leaping, balancing, flipping, rolling—is an example of scientific forces at work. Understanding these forces and the parts they play in executing moves can help gymnasts excel in their sport, moving beyond the basics to more advanced skills.

## EQUIPMENT AND APPARATUSES

There are many distinct kinds of apparatuses new gymnasts will find when they enter a gym, most of which they'll likely learn to use. Throughout a gym, mats are used to protect gymnasts from the hard floor. The mats are located under and around each apparatus and are placed in open areas for floor exercise routines. Without mats, headstands, somersaults, and other moves would certainly be uncomfortable, and a fall off an apparatus could cause injury or even death.

Mats used for gymnastics come in many different sizes, but they do have to meet certain criteria to serve their purpose. They

**TWIST AND TURN** Gymnasts have to stay in a set square area of the floor during their floor exercise routine. The square has sides that are 39.37 feet (12 m) long.

have to be heavy enough that they will not slide away when gymnasts land on them. They also need to be thick enough to provide a cushion when gymnasts land after executing skills that send them airborne. Landing puts major stress on muscles, joints, and bones. Tumbling exercises are tough on the body when a gymnast practices them repeatedly to get them right. A mat helps lessen the impact because it absorbs more of the force from the landing.

The floor used for the floor exercise is different from the other floors and mats around the gym. It is known as a spring floor because it has springs under its top layers. A spring floor exerts a force called spring force on the

Spring floors are used by both male and female gymnasts during their floor exercise routines.

**TWIST AND TURN** Cheerleaders may also use spring floors for practice or competition.

gymnast's body. When a gymnast jumps on this floor, they push the springs down. The springs then push back on the gymnasts' feet with an upward force. This extra push helps gymnasts jump higher, and it protects their legs and feet from absorbing too much of the impact from a landing.

A springboard is another piece of equipment that helps gymnasts. It can be used to launch over the vault, mount the balance beam, or reach the bars. Springboards are made of two boards with several springs between them. They help gymnasts jump higher using the same principle displayed in a spring floor.

## WHY WARM UP?

A gymnast needs to be prepared before they even begin any gymnastics moves. They need to prepare their body by warming up. Warm-up exercises literally warm up the entire body by gradually preparing the body's systems—including the cardiovascular system, respiratory system, and nervous system. The exercises increase blood flow to muscles, warming them up and relaxing tissues so they will stretch more easily.

Gymnasts often do aerobic exercises, such as jogging or jumping rope, to begin warming up. These aerobic activities increase body temperature, heart rate, and circulation. Increased heart rate and circulation cause blood to flow faster, warming muscles and bringing oxygen and nutrients to muscles so the gymnast will have the energy to perform.

After the aerobic portion of a warm-up, gymnasts perform slow stretches to warm up specific areas of the body. They pay special attention to their back and hips, as well as their abdominal, leg, and arm muscles. Gymnasts even stretch and strengthen their feet before an event or a practice. Stretches improve range of motion and condition the tisues surrounding the joints, or the places in the body where bones come together.

No matter the sport, athletes generally warm up before they get to work. Warming up helps prevent injuries and supports peak performance.

Stretches also circulate synovial fluid, a natural lubricant made by the body that helps joints move more easily.

Warming up helps gymnasts perform at their best, and it also helps prevent injury. Gymnasts who do not warm up could easily strain or pull a muscle.

By the end of a warm-up session, gymnasts have changed how their body is functioning. Increased heart rate, breathing rate, and circulation raise body temperature and result in more blood and oxygen reaching the brain, spinal cord, and nerves to produce quicker reactions. The entire nervous system works faster to transmit impulses from the brain and spinal reflex center to muscles. Because of this, the gymnast will be able to move and react faster while performing skills. Vaulting, for example, requires speed to create the force needed to launch the body into the air. Reaction time can also be critical. One example could be when a gymnast has to make a split-second adjustment of positioning in midair while performing on the balance beam.

## ART OF THE FALL

Warming up helps gymnasts prepare their muscles to perform. Still, beginners may move awkwardly at first. After all, even basic skills push new gymnasts into unfamiliar territory. For example, they try out potentially uncomfortable positions when they show off their flexibility on the floor. They also push their body to adapt to heights when they try out the balance beam, rings, and bars.

Nervous gymnasts tense their muscles, so their movements are stiff instead of agile. Stiff, jerky movements make a gymnast more likely to fall. Then, gymnasts who are new to the sport instinctively try to break falls by sticking out their arms. The common result is an injury to the arms, hands, or wrists when the force of impact bends them into dangerous positions. Ligaments may tear, and bones could even break.

In order to combat the problems caused by nervousness, new gymnasts need to gain confidence. Feeling confident helps gymnasts concentrate, relax muscles throughout their body, and conserve energy. When muscles are relaxed, they function more effectively than tight, stiff muscles to help the gymnast create smooth, controlled movements. In the end, relaxed gymnasts are agile and able to perform better and, therefore, not as likely to fall.

Knowing how to fall safely can also help a new gymnast gain courage and confidence. Beginner gymnasts are taught to bring their arms in toward their body instead of out when they fall.

The balance beam requries a strong understanding of how the body is moving without being able to look in a mirror.

With practice, they automatically bend at the hips, knees, and ankles during a fall and roll to the floor to protect their limbs. This technique allows the impact of the fall to be distributed more evenly over the whole body instead of being concentrated on the hands, wrists, and arms. Those extremities can break more easily.

## A SENSE OF SELF

There's a lot to learn when starting gymnastics as a whole or when practicing new moves. Newer gymnasts may not always know what they are doing or how they are moving. This can be another source of anxiety for beginners. They may use their sense of sight to check the positioning of arms, hands, legs, and other body parts. A large wall mirror can help them as they develop their proprioception, or sense of orientation in space. This is also known as kinesthetic awareness.

As beginners practice movements and skills, they improve their ability to understand feedback from proprioceptors, or sensors, in their muscles, joints, ligaments, tendons, and inner ears. Proprioceptors are nerve fibers that detect the motion and position of the body and deliver that information to the central nervous system. With experience, gymnasts gain a sense of what their body is doing as they move, without depending on sight alone.

Gymnasts need to have a strong sense of proprioception. Knowing where their body is and how it is moving without using their eyes keeps them from falling off the balance beam or hurting themselves by moving a body part incorrectly during a flip. It also allows gymnasts to do things such as execute the blind landing that ends the Biles. In fact, pediatrician Carsten Bonnemann stated, "The most beautiful demonstration of proprioception in action is Simone Biles when she is spinning and somersaulting through the air."[11]

New gymnasts also learn to sense their center of gravity and understand how it relates to balance. The center of gravity is the point in a person's body where weight is concentrated so that it is evenly distributed. In order to maintain balance, a gymnast's body weight must be positioned evenly over the supporting body part or parts, such as feet, knees, or hands. As they move, gymnasts continually shift their weight to stay balanced while performing skills.

Beginners start learning balance by working on tumbling exercises, or acrobatic moves performed on the floor. When they crouch to perform rolls, for example, their center of gravity is lower than it is when they are standing. A low center of gravity creates more stability, so they are less likely to fall over. If you see a gymnast bend their knees on the balance beam, they may feel unsteady. That motion brings their center of gravity closer to the beam, making them more stable.

Gymnasts learn to move their body around its axes, which are shown here. This is an example of physics in action!

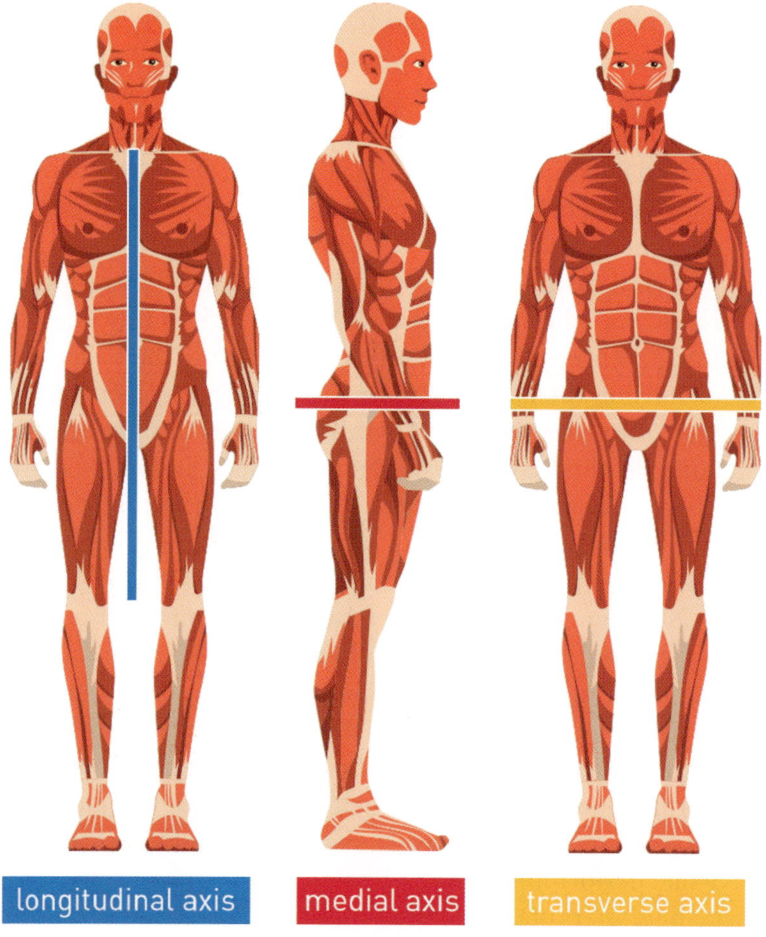


## AROUND THE AXES

Imagine the human body has different imaginary lines running through it. These are axes. The transverse axis runs horizontally across the waist. Somersaults and backflips, among the first new skills a gymnast learns, are performed by

## GYMNASTICS FOR ALL

When Chelsea Werner was born, doctors told her parents she would always have low muscle tone and many other issues. Werner has Down syndrome, a genetic disorder, and one common symptom is low muscle tone. Those who have the disorder may also have other issues such as intellectual and developmental delays. Werner set out at a young age to prove those doctors wrong. She started gymnastics lessons when she was eight years old and never looked back. Today, she's a four-time Special Olympics USA gymnastics champion and a two-time world champion. She also holds several Guinness World Records related to gymnastics. Werner is also a model who's appeared in magazines such as *Teen Vogue* and worked with brands such as Tommy Hilfiger and L'Oreal.

Werner is only one of many gymnasts throughout the world who also has a disability. Gymnasts may have Down syndrome and other disorders, physical differences, and disabilities such as blindness. There are many organizations and adaptations at different levels that can help with training and competition.

As far as international competition, gymnastics has been part of the Special Olympics (for children and adults with intellectual disabilities) since 1972, and there are both rhythmic and artistic categories. However, the Paralympic Games for athletes with physical disabilities do not have gymnastics events as of summer 2025.

rotating the body around the transverse axis. In a front somersault, a gymnast squats on the floor, tucks chin to chest, and rolls forward, returning to the starting position. Gymnasts use proprioception to stay in a straight line so that, eventually, they can perform this skill at a more advanced level, such as on a balance beam. A backflip is just what it sounds like—a flip backward through the air. Beginners are taught to swing their arms back and jump hard to get in the air. Then, the gymnast pushes off the floor with their hands to execute the flip. A spotter can help beginners jump high enough, rotate all the way around the transverse axis, and land on their feet.

Headstands and handstands are beginner skills performed on the longitudinal axis. The longitudinal axis runs vertically from head to toe. In a headstand, gymnasts balance upside down, straighten their legs, and tighten abdominal and back muscles to keep their body in a straight line along the longitudinal axis. Most beginners balance up against a wall first. The wall acts as a support so the gymnast can develop proper form and strengthen the muscles that will eventually help them balance in a freestanding position. The handstand is similar to a headstand, except the gymnast's arms are straight with locked elbows, so all body weight rests on the hands, wrists, and arms. With enough practice, gymnasts eventually learn to walk on their hands. An example of a rotation around the longitudinal axis is a spin that a gymnast performs on the bars or the floor.

A cartwheel is a rotation on the medial axis. The medial axis runs from back to front through the torso. To execute a cartwheel, the gymnast keeps their arms and legs locked straight so the body forms an X shape. Then, the gymnast rotates headfirst either to the left or the right. Body weight is supported on each hand while the gymnast is upside down. The gymnast then quickly rotates back to the starting position.

## WITHOUT THINKING

When people first learn new physical skills, they often must think consciously about the muscles and movements required to perform them. This is certainly true of gymnasts. They are aware of each step it takes to execute a backflip or a cartwheel. With practice, however, muscle memory takes over. Some experts believe that, over time, information about muscle movement becomes an unconscious activity controlled by the part of the brain called the cerebellum. At that point, it could be said that muscle memory begins to work.

Walking is an example of a physical activity controlled by the cerebellum. As babies learn to walk, they struggle to make

# SMALL BUT STRONG

The need for a lower center of gravity is one of the reasons why successful gymnasts tend to be shorter than average people their age. In addition, smaller gymnasts require less force to execute their tricks. Isaac Newton's first law of motion states that an object at rest tends to stay at rest unless acted on by an outside force. This is known as the law of inertia. Objects with more mass have more inertia, which is an object's resistance to a change in its motion. Therefore, in order for a gymnast to begin moving their body or to stop it quickly during a landing, they must create enough force to overcome their body's inertia. The more inertia they have, the more force is needed to overcome it. This is why it is good for gymnasts to be small enough to have less inertia than other athletes but not so small that they cannot generate enough force to properly propel their body into action or stop it once it is moving.

Smaller gymnasts also benefit from having shorter limbs. Gymnasts often try to perform multiple rotations of their body in the air before landing. To do this, they pull their limbs in as close to the axis of rotation as possible. Having shorter limbs allows them to do this more easily.

It is helpful for gymnasts to be small in stature, but they also need to be strong. Simone Biles, for example, is known for her powerful muscles!

Gravity is working to bring this gymnast back toward the ground. Her job is to catch herself on the bar so she doesn't hit the mat.

their muscles move where they want to go. Adults, however, do not have to focus their energy and concentrate in order to walk down the street. They have been walking for so long that they just do it without consciously considering each muscle they need to move. For gymnasts, muscle memory is important because their tumbling passes, balance beam routines, and vaults are incredibly complex. For example, a gymnast may have to execute a series of backflips in a short period of time during a floor exercise routine. They cannot spend time consciously thinking about every movement to do one.

## FORCES OF NATURE

Gymnasts also do not usually think about the forces acting on their body while they are executing their moves. A force is any push or pull on an object. One force that is always at work on a gymnast's body is gravity. This is the force that acts on all things on Earth, pulling objects and living things toward the center of the planet. Gravity is also the force that keeps Earth in orbit around the sun.

Gymnasts are often said to defy gravity because of how long they stay in the air while executing tricks. How do they accomplish this? They use another kind of force to push themselves off the mat or another apparatus and into motion in the air. This kind of force is called applied force. An applied force—as its name suggests—is a force that is applied to an object, such as a gymnast's hands pushing off the floor before a flip. Gymnasts use applied force every time they push off the floor with their hands or feet to jump or flip.

Forces can be seen in action in nearly every aspect of a gymnastics competition. No matter how superhuman they may seem, gymnasts are still at the mercy of forces such as gravity. They have simply trained their bodies to work against that force for as long as possible until it inevitably pulls them back to the ground for their landing. Experienced gymnasts know how to best generate more force with their body. This allows them to stay in the air longer and execute more complex flips and other moves during that time.

# CHAPTER THREE

# FLYING HIGH

If a gymnast continues to work, learn, and train, they'll likely start working on more difficult moves. Advanced skills including tumbling passes, flips off the bars, and high-flying vaults are strong examples of science at work. Gymnasts may not think about the scientific concepts being demonstrated as they fly through the air, but that does not mean these concepts should be ignored. Instead, we can study them closely in order to better understand and appreciate how gymnasts can soar to new heights.

## VELOCITY AND ACCELERATION

Gymnasts are always moving. Nowhere is that more clearly seen than during the floor exercise. During this event, gymnasts often take big running starts before executing tricks, changing their position on the floor very quickly. The rate at which an object—or, in this case, a person—changes its position is known as velocity. A change in velocity is known as acceleration, and gymnasts accelerate as they get ready to execute tumbling passes or vaults. Acceleration is important for gymnasts because it allows them to push off with more force to execute their tricks. This is explained by Newton's second law of motion, which states that force is equal to an object's mass multiplied by its acceleration.

When commentators, coaches, fans, and even gymnasts themselves talk about a gymnast's velocity, they often use the word "speed" instead. However, there is an important difference between speed and velocity. Direction does not matter when measuring speed but matters when measuring velocity.

Each amazing skill that gymnasts demonstrate involves scientific principles being put into action.

Velocity is determined in part by how far an object is from its starting position.

Accelerating into advanced skills can be scary for gymnasts, but running fast enough toward the vault and across the floor is the only way to get enough power to execute the most challenging moves. As Olympic champion gymnast Mary Lou Retton said, "It can be frightening running full speed, knowing that if you mess up you're going to crash into the [vault]. So I can see where people get intimidated by it … But you still have to go full out because speed is the key. You're going horizontal and suddenly you have to punch it and go vertical, so you need all the momentum you can get."[12] Because momentum is the result of mass multiplied by velocity, it is important for gymnasts—especially smaller gymnasts—to run fast.

## FOR SAFETY'S SAKE

Today's vaulting tables are safer for gymnasts.

Within the past 20 years, the rules for the design and use of gymnastics apparatuses have changed to make them safer for athletes. For example, gymnasts used to perform vaults using the pommel horse with its handles removed. Doing tricks over the horse was dangerous, even in practice. "The horse used to be long and skinny, with only a limited space to put your hands. When you are doing a flip-flop onto it, you basically have to go to the right spot every single time, and that was a little scary," Olympic gymnast Carly Patterson told *TIME* magazine in 2008. "A lot of times, I would see people's hands slipping off, or missing the horse completely."[1]

In 2001, the horse was replaced with the wider and safer vaulting table used today. The greater surface area of the vaulting table gives gymnasts more places to put their hands, reducing the probability that they will miss the table after jumping off the springboard. The front of the table is curved downward to prevent broken bones if a gymnast misses jumping over the table and instead hits the front of it.

Rules have also changed to require a mat in front of the vault. The mat surrounds the springboard where gymnasts launch into the air. It can provide protection in case gymnasts slip or fall.

Some people in the gymnastics community would like to see more steps taken to prepare athletes and make the sport safer. "There are a lot of things that have been done to make gymnastics safer, but you can always do more,"[2] said Olympic gymnast Shannon Miller.

1. Quoted in Alice Park, "Making Gymnastics Safer for Kids," *TIME*, April 8, 2008. www.time.com/time/health/article/0,8599,1728902,00.html.
2. Quoted in Park, "Making Gymnastics Safer for Kids."

## SCIENCE IN ACTION

Gymnasts show off Newton's laws in every event, but the vault is an excellent way to see them in action, especially his second and third laws. Newton's second law can be seen both in the need for acceleration to increase the force when gymnasts push off the vaulting table and in the way the force applied to the table helps a gymnast accelerate in the air. This is because the second law also states that acceleration increases when force increases.

In addition, when a gymnast touches a surface, such as the vaulting table, Newton's third law of motion is at work. This law states that for every action, there is an equal and opposite reaction. When gymnasts push down on the vaulting table with their hands, the vault does not collapse through the floor. Instead, it pushes up with an equal and opposite force. That force helps launch gymnasts into the air.

Writing for the *Huffington Post*, Sarah Sloat described the relationship between Newton's second and third laws and the success of a gymnast's vault:

> *Getting the right height is an exercise in physics reliant on strength. Gymnasts have to reach a maximum velocity on their approach to the springboard to get maximum force—the more mass and acceleration used, the more air they are going to get. That's in line with Newton's second law while his third law (for every action, there is an equal but opposite reaction) explains why the exertion of force on the springboard is what enables the athlete to propel into the air. More air time affects the rotational velocity of the gymnast …*[13]

If a gymnast does not use the right amount of force according to these two laws, it negatively affects their vault. They can push off with too much force, throwing off their rotation in the air and making landing difficult or dangerous. They also can push off with not enough force, failing to get enough height to execute the skill correctly. Both of these issues can also lead to injury.

Shown here is a gymnast executing a vault. This gymnastics event relies on the application of many physics principles to ensure a gymnast's safety and success.

**TWIST AND TURN** Gymnasts usually sprint about 82 feet (25 m) before a vault.

## OPPOSING FORCES

Kinetic energy is the energy of motion. It's not easy to stop once an object gets moving. Still, while gymnasts try to accelerate, other forces work to slow them down. Gymnasts fight against friction, which is a force that exists when an object moves across a surface and generally works to slow down an object's motion. They also fight drag, or air resistance, which is a form of friction created when air particles come in contact with the gymnast's body. More force pushing objects together means more friction will result, such as during a vault when gymnasts touch the floor with their feet and push off the vault with their hands. The force at these points of contact creates friction and resistance that slows gymnasts down.

Although friction and drag can be negative forces when gymnasts are trying to move as quickly as possible, they can also be beneficial and even lifesaving in other circumstances. In fact, in many events, gymnasts try to create friction to keep themselves from slipping on the apparatus, which could cause point deductions or serious injuries. They use many different sticky substances to create friction. Chalk is a popular choice for gymnasts looking to keep themselves from losing their grip, and some mix it with water or honey. Throughout the history of the sport, other gymnasts have used more creative options to increase friction, including soda, maple syrup, and melted gummy bears. This is allowed as long as it doesn't leave a mess.

## ANGLES IN THE AIR

When gymnasts become airborne, they have to work against air resistance and find ways to execute multiple rotations of their body in the air. Gymnasts may push off from a standing position or gain momentum from turns on the bar, then let go to become airborne. As gymnasts launch into the air in a spin off the uneven bars, they use angular momentum, which is

Chalk is used by many gymnasts to create the friction necessary to hold on to pieces of equipment. Without enough friction to keep their hands from slipping, a gymnast could fall off the apparatus and get seriously injured.

## THE BEAR AND THE BARS

Some male gymnasts keep an unusual buddy with them as they prepare for their parallel bars routine—a honey bear. Honey is often sold in bottles that look like bears, and these containers have become common sights around elite gymnastics competitions. The natural stickiness of honey makes it a good choice for increasing friction between a gymnast's hands and the parallel bars. Some gymnasts, such as Chris Brooks and Danell Leyva, have mixed honey and chalk to create the perfect friction-reducing substance.

"Chalk and honey is the best thing you have for holding on ... Just regular honey,"[1] Brooks said before the 2016 Olympic Games.

There is another advantage of using honey, according to Geoffrey A. Fowler of the *Wall Street Journal*: "It doubles as a tasty treat."[2]

1. Quoted in Julia Fincher, "Have Chalk, Will Travel: Why Gymnasts Brought Their Own Chalk to Rio,"NBCOlympics.com, August 16, 2016. www.nbcolympics.com/news/have-chalk-will-travel-whygymnasts-brought-their-own-chalk-rio.
2. Geoffrey A. Fowler, "Honey, Here's a Gripping Tale: How Olympians Hang On to the Bar," *The Wall Street Journal*, July 22, 2012. www.wsj.com/articles SB10000872396390 444097904577535700455486064.

the rotational momentum of a body that is turning around an axis. Once gymnasts are in the air, angular momentum remains constant. It cannot be increased or decreased because there is nothing solid in the air to push off from.

Still, gymnasts need a way to accelerate so they can spin and flip while airborne. They need to increase their spinning speed, or angular velocity, by pulling their limbs in and creating a more compact shape, which is less resistant to acceleration and less impacted by air resistance. The speed of spinning can be calculated by dividing the measurement of a circle by the time it takes to complete a full revolution. There are 360 degrees in a circle. A gymnast who completes one revolution (360 degrees) in four seconds is spinning at a rate of 90 degrees per second.

## ON THE FLY

There are other challenges gymnasts encounter when performing airborne moves. Naturally, they must take their eyes off

## THE PRODUNOVA

At the 2016 Olympic Games, two female gymnasts attempted a vault that was nicknamed the "vault of death" because of how dangerous it is. Its real name is the Produnova, named after Russian gymnast Yelena Produnova, and it involves doing a front handspring onto the vaulting table and then executing two somersaults before landing. This combination of skills can be dangerous for multiple reasons, according to journalist Hannah Orenstein: "The Produnova is among the most extreme moves a gymnast can attempt in a sport full of extremely dangerous stunts. If the athlete rotates too far forward, she can break her legs. If she doesn't rotate far enough, she can break her neck."[1]

These risks proved to be too much for Team USA, and none of the U.S. gymnasts attempted the trick at the 2016 Olympic Games. However, Oksana Chusovitina of Uzbekistan and Dipa Karmakar of India both attempted it in Olympic competition that year. Chusovitina landed with another somersault on the ground, while Karmakar landed on her feet but received a small deduction for her bottom touching the ground afterward.

Karmakar understood the risks involved in attempting this trick, once saying, "One wrong move and I could die on the spot."[2] However, she successfully landed the move in April 2016, on her way to becoming India's first female gymnast to qualify for Olympic competition. In doing so, she became one of only a small group of women to successfully execute the "vault of death." She retired in 2024.

1. Hannah Orenstein, "You Need to See the Death-Defying Move This Gymnast Just Barely Pulls Off," *Seventeen*, June 28, 2016.www.seventeen.com/life/a41454/dipa-karmakar-produnova-vault/.
2. Quoted in Orenstein, "You Need to See the Death-Defying Move This Gymnast Just Barely Pulls Off."

the apparatus they are using to perform flips and rotations. To complete the move, they must relocate the apparatus while in motion and land flawlessly to maintain their rhythm and continue their routine. For example, when gymnasts perform aerial skills such as front flips and backflips on the beam, they have to figure out how to land back on the beam before they actually see it. This is where proprioception is most important for gymnasts.

As of 2025, Dipa Karmakar, who is shown here, remains one of only five women who have successfully executed the Produnova.

**TWIST AND TURN** Simone Biles has the highest recorded score in women's gymnastics vault: 15.633 in 2022.

Former Olympic gymnast Kurt Thomas explained, "If you depend on your eyes to tell you where you are, all you see is a blur of walls, lights, and faces. Some gymnasts count to themselves, 'One … two … three,' in order to anticipate their landing. But over the years I seem to have acquired an air sense of where I am at all times during a trick."[14]

Proprioception also helps elite gymnasts stay oriented while adjusting their form and body positioning in the air. According to Nadia Comăneci, aerials on the beam are a particularly difficult skill to master and require a strong sense of body awareness while in the air. "I always knew when I was crooked going into an aerial on the beam," she has said. "Just like all elite gymnasts, I'd make tiny corrections while in the air. Those split-second judgments made the difference between falling off the beam and hurting myself or completing a successful skill that allowed me to win competitions."[15]

Tiny corrections and split-second judgments are determining factors in competitions at the highest levels. Winning requires performing with absolute precision. Throughout an entire routine or even during one trick, elite gymnasts have to get each move right from beginning to end. They work to perfect timing, body positioning, speed, and momentum while in the air. They also have to adjust each element based on how a move progresses in the moment. As Mary Lou Retton has said, "Every little mistake—a wobble on the beam, a hop on the landing, a slipped hand on the bars—can cost you a tenth of a point, and in our sport, that's the difference between first and second [place]."[16] Proprioception allows gymnasts to notice by the feeling in their body if something is off, which helps them correct themselves. The correction keeps them from losing points for mistakes, but more importantly it can keep them from getting hurt.

Male and female gymnasts learn to sense their body's movements so they can land safely.

## LEGENDARY LANDING

Even under the worst circumstances, elite gymnasts are prepared to do whatever they can to stick their landing. They practice landings over and over, and they know what to do to save their score and their body when a perfect landing is impossible. When Kerri Strug performed her gold-medal vault at the 1996 Olympic Games, she had a severe ankle injury. She kept going, made decisions based on the circumstances, and managed to stick her landing. She described what happened in her book *Landing on My Feet: A Diary of Dreams:*

> *I slammed into the floor a little short [of the proper position], but clean, and immediately, I heard another big rip in my ankle. I thought for sure my leg had snapped in two … Instinctively, maybe because I had done it thousands of times since the first time [my sister] Lisa showed me when I was three years old, I hopped into the finishing pose. I did it standing on just my right foot, like a flamingo. But I threw my shoulders back, stuck out my chin, stretched out my arms, and saluted the judges.*[1]

1. Kerri Strug and John P. Lopez, *Landing on My Feet: A Diary of Dreams*. Kansas City, MO: Andrews McMeel, 1997, p. 169.

## STICK THE LANDING

A gymnastics routine's final element is the dismount, or landing. Gymnasts must "stick" their landings to earn good scores in competition. That means landing on their feet and stopping their motion immediately. Even when dismounting from an apparatus such as the vault, bars, or beam, they cannot hop around or take a step to stabilize their bodies without some kind of deduction.

Newton's first law of motion—an object in motion tends to stay in motion—is one reason landing from an airborne trick is so difficult. When a gymnast's body is in motion, it wants to stay in motion, so it requires extra force to stop as quickly as gymnasts need to.

Elite gymnasts struggle with landings just like less-experienced gymnasts. In fact, top gymnasts have to work even

Kerri Strug, shown here, had one of the most famous landings in the history of her sport.

harder to control landing forces because their tricks require more angular velocity, they reach greater heights, and they gain more momentum as they perform their moves. These factors contribute to the strong forces at play as a gymnast lands, which must be controlled to execute a proper landing. Landing hard at the end of a trick produces forces that can knock gymnasts off balance and cause injury.

When gymnasts prepare to dismount from an apparatus, they use angular momentum just like they did at the beginning of their routine. This time, however, they need to decrease their angular velocity to gain control over their landing. They stretch their body open to increase the distance between their center of gravity and the axis of movement. This slows them down, so they can spend more time in the air before hitting the mat on the ground.

Gymnasts take that time to prepare for their landing. In a split second, gymnasts adjust their body so they will land with their center of gravity best positioned for balance. They are less likely to be thrown off balance if landing forces are distributed evenly throughout their body. In many cases, if a gymnast does not perfectly stick their landing, they step in the direction they were moving in before they landed. This is also explained using Newton's first law of motion. It states that objects in motion want to continue their motion with the same velocity, which means in the same direction.

To achieve a stable position when landing, gymnasts bend at the knees, ankles, and hips as they hit the mat. This way, they're better able to absorb the impact of the landing forces before straightening up to a standing position without otherwise moving. Then, in competition, they're generally required to salute the judges by holding their arms up. After that, they're done!

# CHAPTER FOUR

# TRAINING TRIALS

You've read about how elite gymnasts accomplish some of the feats that make their events so popular at each Olympic Summer Games. They train intensely for many years to develop the strength and flexibility needed to perform at the highest level. This training is not easy on a gymnast's body. Some people tend to dismiss gymnasts as "not real athletes" because their sport has judges, but this intense training makes gymnasts much tougher athletes than they often get credit for being.

"I always thought gymnastics is one of the hardest sports, if not the hardest," Carly Patterson once said. "The amount of hours we train, it's a lot for your body."[17]

Science plays an important part in training for gymnasts. In order to create a beneficial training program that prepares gymnasts for success but does not push their body too hard, both the athletes and their coaches need a strong understanding of the human body and how its many systems work together.

This balance is also important when it comes to what gymnasts eat as they are training. A healthy diet is necessary for athletes to help them perform at their highest level, so gymnasts and those who help them prepare their meals must have a good sense of what foods will provide the nutrients they need to be in their best shape. Gymnasts—especially female gymnasts—are typically smaller athletes, but it is important that the focus remains on a gymnast being healthy and strong instead of too thin.

Gymnasts need to strengthen all their major muscle groups to pull off the skills needed to succeed.

All elite gymnasts need to be strong. Intense training helps them develop that strength. It is only after years of training that gymnasts are able to demonstrate the most amazing airborne skills and meet all the exacting standards of their sport.

## OVER AND OVER AGAIN

Gymnasts must focus on practicing the same skills again and again. Repetition helps gymnasts move ahead in the sport in part because practice trains the brain. With every repetition of a move, the brain learns to use more parts of muscles and to use muscles in new ways so they are more efficient. Practice also improves flexibility and strengthens the muscles required for specific skills.

Gymnastics workouts can be intense, whether gymnasts are just starting out, veterans of the sport, or trying to make a comeback. Many gymnasts start young and train for more than 30 hours each week. In some cases, young gymnasts are homeschooled to give them more time to train. This helps with their development as athletes, but it can cause them to miss out on some of the social aspects of young adult life. However, many successful elite gymnasts believe the sacrifices they made to train as hard as they did were worth it. For example, Simone Biles's mother, Nellie, recalled her daughter once telling her:

> *Well, Mom … I have lost so much. By giving up public school, I lost a lot of friends because we don't have the same interests. I don't do this "hanging out," whatever that is. I've never gone to someone's party, so I don't know what they do there. And I've never gone to a homecoming; never a prom.*
>
> *I gave up a lot, but I made the right decision because look what I've accomplished.*[18]

Most gymnasts begin training at a very young age.

# WHAT TO WEAR

Whether warming up, working out, or competing, gymnasts wear specific outfits to enhance their performance. Female gymnasts traditionally wear a long-sleeved leotard. They are also allowed to wear a sleeveless leotard in competition. Male gymnasts traditionally wear a sleeveless leotard with shorts or pants depending on the event. These leotards are made of stretchy fabric, so they will not hinder gymnasts' movements. The outfits are tight, so coaches and judges can see how gymnasts move and create body shapes.

Gymnasts' outfits are designed with science in mind too. Heavier clothing could weigh gymnasts down when they attempt to launch into the air, and that would mean more force would be required when they jump. Looser clothing could disrupt the airflow around the gymnast as they perform tricks, creating drag that would slow them down as they run and leap through the air. Tight clothing helps gymnasts create an aerodynamic shape with their body, so they can move through the air more easily. Air flows with less resistance over a body that is sleek and smooth.

Gymnasts' leotards are not just stylish; they're also scientific!

## STRETCHING SKILLS

Stretching can help anyone become a bit more flexible and gain a better range of motion. However, gymnastics requires athletes to have a range of motion that's beyond the usual. For example, most people who are not gymnasts cannot perform a straddle split, which requires sitting with the legs to the sides of the body 180 degrees apart. In order to work up to such a skill, every gymnast has a workout schedule that includes flexibility training. Stretches help increase flexibility throughout the body, including in the hip flexors, in the shoulders, and even in the fingers and toes. Stretching conditions not only the muscles, but also the tendons and ligaments that support joints, so they are prepared for gymnastic moves and become less prone to injury.

Static stretches, or stretches in which people hold their body in one position for a certain length of time, are often used to improve flexibility. For example, in a static stretch to improve the straddle split, gymnasts sit in the split position with their legs as far out as they will go. In a dynamic stretch, gymnasts do the same, then contract their muscles and pull their legs back even further. They relax and then repeat the contraction, pulling back over and over to increase the stretch. The increase in flexibility comes from muscle tissue adapting to the stretching movements. Over time, the muscle develops into longer tissue, increasing overall flexibility.

## MUSCLE MOVEMENTS

A gymnast needs excellent muscle strength to perform moves well. Many gymnastic skills require quick bursts of intense energy to launch, twist, and flip in the air. For these types of skills, gymnasts need to develop fast-twitch muscle fibers. When they sprint toward the vault, for example, fast-twitch muscle fibers respond to nerve impulses from the brain by contracting quickly and forcefully. The fast muscle movement creates velocity, and the force of the contraction creates power.

Gymnasts condition fast-twitch muscle fibers through plyometric drills, such as jumps, which rapidly stretch and contract the muscles with added force to increase muscle power. Plyometric drills are meant to overload muscle. This stimulates the brain to recruit more fast-twitch muscle fibers to work. With more fast-twitch muscle in use, a gymnast will gain speed and power and perform more efficiently.

Gymnasts also focus on strengthening their core muscles, which are needed for every move—from pulling up on the bars to flipping on the balance beam. The core muscles include the abdominals and other muscles that stabilize the torso from the shoulders to the pelvis and along the spine. When gymnasts

Athletes in a variety of sports perform plyometric drills. This is because most sports use fast-twitch muscle fibers.

**TWIST AND TURN** In 1963, USA Gymnastics was established to oversee gymnastics in the United States. Its responsibilities include setting rules, educating coaches, and selecting and training gymnasts for the Olympic Games and World Championships.

perform a handstand, for example, they tighten their core muscles to balance and hold their body in a straight line without tipping forward, backward, or to the side. Gymnasts strengthen these muscles through exercises such as sit-ups, crunches, and V-sits. In V-sits, gymnasts lie on their back with their legs straight. They use their abdominal muscles to lift their legs to a 45-degree angle. Then, they reach forward toward their shins for a deeper contraction. With their body in a V shape, gymnasts can work their rectus abdominus muscle (sometimes just called the abdominals or abs), obliques, and hip flexors.

Soreness is normal when muscles are challenged to the point of fatigue. They're slightly injured in the process, and new cells repair them, making them stronger. However, gymnasts must be careful not to do too much too fast, which damages muscles.

## KEEP GOING

Flexibility and muscle strength are important. However, gymnasts also need endurance. Without endurance, they lose energy, which means they lose the physical capacity to do work. In that case, they cannot perform well, even during a floor routine that lasts only 60 to 90 seconds.

Athletes use slow-twitch muscle fibers to perform physical activity for long periods of time. Compared to fast-twitch muscle fibers, slow-twitch muscle fibers contract more slowly, but they do not get fatigued as quickly as fast-twitch muscle fibers. That is what makes them the building blocks for endurance. Slow-twitch muscle fibers are used during exercises such as long-distance running and cycling. Through prolonged cardiovascular exercise, the muscles adapt to the work and become better able to tolerate activities that require a greater amount of endurance.

## EATING AND HYDRATING

It's very important for gymnasts to avoid dehydration, especially around training and competition. Muscle tissue needs water to function, since it is made of about 75 percent water. Dehydration can adversely affect mental concentration, how the body regulates temperature, and muscular performance. Taking in small amounts of fluid throughout a workout session helps gymnasts replenish fluids lost through sweating.

Gymnasts also know they have to provide the fuel that will get their body through an intense workout. Fuel for a gymnast's body means eating foods that contain proteins and carbohydrates. Without the proper nutrients, gymnasts cannot build the muscles they need to perform. Their body will be weak and lack energy, endurance, and power.

In order to provide fast-twitch muscle fibers with the glycogen they use for energy, gymnasts need to eat carbohydrates. Carbohydrates break down during digestion and create sugars, including glycogen, in the body. There are two types of carbohydrates: simple and complex. Simple carbohydrates break down very quickly and are found in foods and drinks such as baked goods and fruit juices. They provide a burst of energy that does not last long. Gymnasts benefit more by loading up on complex carbohydrates, which are found in whole grains and vegetables, among other healthy foods. Complex carbohydrates break down more slowly, so the energy they provide lasts longer.

Gymnasts also get energy from lean protein, which is found in sources such as fish and chicken. During digestion, protein is broken down into amino acids. Amino acids are used to build and replenish the muscle tissue gymnasts need to perform tricks. Excess amino acids are metabolized into glycogen, which can be used for energy. Protein is also converted into adenosine triphosphate (ATP), a source of energy for muscles.

Today's Olympic gymnasts carefully structure their diets to make sure they are getting the proper amount of protein and carbohydrates. They eat foods such as bananas, oatmeal, rice, vegetables, grilled chicken, and salmon to give their

Gymnasts need to make sure they are eating enough food to have the energy to train. This is especially important for young gymnasts who are still growing.

**TWIST AND TURN** Athletes can lose 2 quarts (1.9 L) of fluid (and salt) or more for every hour of exercise. Endurance athletes can lose 3 quarts (2.8 L) or more.

body energy as they train. As Olympic gymnast Aly Raisman said, "Everything I eat is meant to fuel and take care of my body."[19]

Although elite gymnasts' main focus is on eating nutrient-dense foods, they still allow themselves to have treats such as chocolate. For example, Olympic champion Gabby Douglas was known to treat herself to gingerbread after a day of training. It's not healthy to completely deny yourself any kind of food, especially foods that bring you joy.

## YOUNG GYMNASTS

Many of the best gymnasts begin training when they're very young. Simone Biles was first exposed to gymnastics as a six year old, and she never looked back. She had been performing her own flips and tricks around the house long before that, but formal training helped her channel that energy into something productive and successful.

Gymnasts generally start training before they reach puberty. Many coaches believe that childhood is a good time to maximize their potential because gymnasts have less body mass than they will have when they grow up. Body mass refers to how much space a gymnast's body occupies as well as how much they weigh. It takes less energy for lighter, more streamlined gymnasts to launch into the air to perform tricks. Because younger, smaller gymnasts have less surface area, they also encounter less resistance as they move through the air. Also, when smaller gymnasts land, they create less force upon impact, allowing them to maintain their balance better.

Some people in the gymnastics community believe younger gymnasts also have less experience with failure and fear and may not fully understand the physical risks they are taking. This

# NO SHAME IN ADHD

After the 2016 Olympic Games, hackers released medical records from various U.S. Olympic athletes, looking to discredit them by showing that they were taking banned substances. One of the athletes whose medical records were leaked was Simone Biles. It was revealed that she had been taking a banned substance to treat attention-deficit/hyperactivity disorder (ADHD), a disorder that affects up to 11 percent of children in the United States. However, USA Gymnastics proved that Biles had received formal permission to take the substance for medical reasons.

Biles took to social media after the leak. In a pair of posts, she stated:

> *I have ADHD and I have taken medicine for it since I was a kid. Please know, I believe in a clean sport, have always followed the rules, and will continue to do so as fair play is critical to sport and is very important to me … Having ADHD, and taking medicine for it is nothing to be ashamed of nothing that I'm afraid to let people know.*[1]

Many famous Olympians, including legendary swimmer Michael Phelps, were diagnosed with ADHD as children. Sports can help children with ADHD channel their excess energy and can help them feel as if their disorder does not define them. In fact, ADHD can actually be helpful in some sports, including gymnastics. As ESPNW contributor Aimee Crawford wrote:

> *The impulsivity and fearlessness common in kids with ADHD also comes in handy in individual sports like martial arts or gymnastics, wthere ADHD isn't a hindrance, but perhaps a superpower. The key—as with all superpowers—is learning to harness it.*[2]

Biles learned to harness her superpower, and her openness about living with ADHD has acted as another kind of superpower, inspiring young people with the disorder to believe they, too, can achieve great things.

1. Quoted in Aimee Crawford, "Bravo, Simone Biles, for Taking a Stand Against ADHD Stigma," ESPNW, September 21, 2016. www.espn.com/espnw/voices/article/17602540/bravo-simone-biles-takingstand-adhd-stigma.
2. Crawford, "Bravo, Simone Biles."

makes them more willing to try certain tricks without anything mentally holding them back.

Young gymnasts have to sacrifice physically, psychologically, and socially for their sport, and this can leave them feeling drained as they get older. Gymnasts often retire at a relatively young age because they spent so much of their childhood dedicating their body, mind, and time to the sport. As journalist Liz Clarke wrote:

> *It's not simply that the high-risk stunts demand feather-light, pre-pubescent physiques. They also demand single-minded focus. For many female gymnasts, after sacrificing so much of their adolescence—eschewing summer camps, slumber parties and proms for so many years—it's difficult to keep sacrificing after their Olympic dream comes true.*[20]

However, gymnasts such as Simone Biles are challenging this idea. Biles has been open about finding ways to balance her love for her sport with her desire to enjoy life outside of that sport as she has gotten older. She has also discussed the importance of protecting her mental health by taking breaks from the sport if it is causing her too much stress and anxiety. By prioritizing her mental and emotional needs, she has continued to excel in the sport long after the age at which many gymnasts retire.

## TOO MUCH TRAINING?

Top gymnasts today train for hours almost every day. They often train between 25 and 40 hours each week. They practice skills and routines over and over so the moves become natural and require less energy to perform. They also work with sports psychologists to prepare for the pressure of competing.

Some gymnasts become so dedicated to the sport that they take extreme measures to stay competitive. They might train more vigorously than their body can handle, risking injury to muscles, joints, and bones. Although there are examples of coaches who encourage this kind of dangerous training, most put their athletes' health first. Leading up to the 2008 Olympic

Shawn Johnson has spoken openly about the pressure felt by many female gymnasts to be as thin as possible.

Games, American gymnast Shawn Johnson trained 10 to 15 fewer hours each week than elite gymnasts traditionally trained. That kept her from burning out physically or emotionally, and she won four medals at those Games.

Elite gymnasts, especially female gymnasts, also have a reputation of developing eating disorders as they try to stay as light and lean as children so they will be more competitive. To keep themselves from gaining weight—or even entering puberty—some have starved themselves. Other gymnasts have developed the habit of purging or abusing laxatives to keep their body from fully digesting the food they eat. This type of dangerous behavior can lead to serious health complications and even death.

Although Shawn Johnson's training schedule was admirable during the lead-up to the 2008 Olympic Games, her diet was something no one should emulate. She has admitted that she would often eat as few as 700 calories a day; a healthy calorie intake is more than double that amount. A *People* magazine story in 2015 detailed the gymnast's struggle with her body image and the expectations placed on her to live up to the ideal gymnast body type:

> *Johnson's desire to be thinner came from what she thought judges expected from a gymnast. "Back then, the judges liked the look of a very lean and skinny gymnast that was artistic and graceful, rather than powerful like myself," she says, adding that she felt immense pressure to transform her body into what it was not.*[21]

Many gymnasts throughout the history of the sport have felt the same pressure as Johnson to be as thin as possible. However, many of today's successful gymnasts are known less for how thin they are than for how muscular they are. As Johnson said before the 2016 Olympic Games, "The prospects going to Rio are the stronger types, the muscular and powerful girls."[22] Simone Biles, one of the greatest gymnasts and Olympians of all time at this point, is known for her muscular build and strength training, something that has paid off in 11 Olympic medals.

## HEALTHY AND STRONG

Human bodies are all different. They have different bends and curves. These curves and differences can affect a gymnast's performance. Objects that are not streamlined create air resistance and drag, which slows their motion through space. A small body type, however, does not always provide a competitive edge for gymnasts. The lack of larger muscles can actually be a disadvantage in performing skills that require speed and power. For example, gymnasts use their muscles to gain speed when running toward the vault. This helps them launch into the air and gain distance and height. Height is needed to perform flips

The U.S. women's gymnastics team that competed at the 2024 Olympics was a team of strong, powerful athletes.

## PRIDE IN STRENGTH

In 2016, Olympic gymnast Aly Raisman took to the social media platform Instagram to share pictures of herself with her muscular arms clearly visible. She wrote a caption for the images that focused on her acceptance of her own physical strength after being shamed for it while growing up:

> *Shoutout to all the boys from 5th–9th grade who made fun of me for being "too strong." Thanks for forcing me to learn to love myself and my body. My muscular arms that were considered weird and gross when I was younger have made me one of the best gymnasts on the planet. Don't ever let anyone tell you how you should or shouldn't look. There is no such thing as a perfect body type.*[1]

1. Quoted in Rose Minutaglio, "Simone Biles on Overcoming Body-Shaming from Coach: 'It Just TaughtMe to Rise Above," *People*, November 16, 2016. people.com/sports/simone-biles-on-overcoming-bodyshaming-from-coach-it-just-taught-me-to-rise-above/.

and twists properly before landing, and gymnasts are judged on the distance and height they achieve. A more impressive performance will earn them points in competition regardless of their size.

The 2024 Golden Girls have become role models for young gymnasts—and all young people—to appreciate their bodies for what they do instead of what they look like. Simone Biles has spoken out publicly about the body shaming she has faced for having a more muscular build than many female gymnasts. However, she has also said, "I was born with my body for a reason and I'm using it to compete in the sport that I love."[23]

Biles and her teammates believe that there is no one "right" body for a gymnast to have, and they are living proof of that. "We're all born with unique bodies, and we've proved that you can have any type of body and be good,"[24] Biles said.

Body type and size are not the sole determining factors for success in gymnastics, and gymnasts never need to abuse their body to win. Working out and eating healthy foods can help gymnasts excel, but care must be taken to prioritize the gymnast's health above all else. A strong gymnast is a successful gymnast. The Golden Girls have the medals to prove it.

# CHAPTER FIVE

# SCIENCE OF SAFETY

Gymnastics sometimes isn't taken seriously, perhaps because it's a sport that attracts many young girls. However, this attitude is incorrect; it's an extremely tough sport. It is physically demanding and puts a lot of stress on an athlete's body. Although gymnasts often make what they do look easy, they are not safe from injury. In fact, according to the first comprehensive study of gymnastics injuries in the United States, gymnasts are just as likely as basketball players, ice hockey players, and soccer players to sustain an injury.

The likelihood of injury is something that should be taken very seriously. As former Olympic champion Shannon Miller stated:

> *You can't play at gymnastics … You shouldn't do pick-up gymnastics in your backyard. If you're doing it right, everything from your little toe to your little finger is constantly in motion. Everything is flipping, moving, or turning. It works the entire body in a way no other sport does, and the more body parts that are moving, the more you are open to injuries. So, safety should absolutely be the number-one concern.*[25]

The best way to prevent and treat injuries in gymnastics is to understand them on a scientific level. This is a sport that can take a toll on the body and the mind, so knowledge of the physical and psychological effects of the sport on athletes is very important. Educated athletes are better prepared to stay safe and become successful.

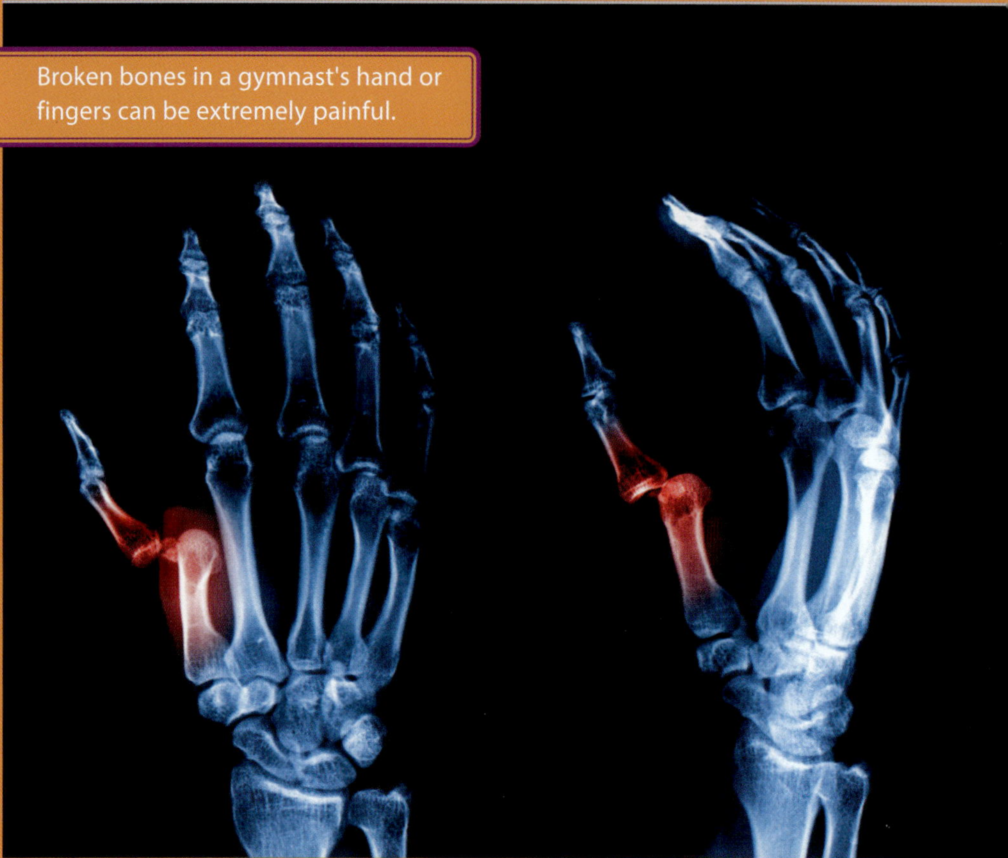

Broken bones in a gymnast's hand or fingers can be extremely painful.

## CARE FOR EXTREMITIES

When beginner gymnasts injure themselves, these injuries are generally minor and often to their hands or feet. For example, when gymnasts are in motion, they can easily catch a finger on an apparatus. Due to momentum and Newton's first law of motion (an object in motion tends to stay in motion), the gymnast's body will keep moving forward while the finger is caught. That can result in a dislocation, which means the bone is pushed out of position at the joint. It could also result in a broken finger.

A dislocated finger looks deformed, but it can often be pulled back into place. If the finger is broken, the gymnast will feel even more pain and can expect swelling, too. A lot of swelling may cause numbness, as nerves in the hand are

**TWIST AND TURN** A report on injuries to college athletes showed that gymnastics injuries were second only to those in wrestling. Even football players had fewer injuries.

compressed. A broken finger can be diagnosed by an X-ray and may need a splint to hold it still while it heals.

The effects of friction also cause minor injuries to beginners as well as more experienced gymnasts. When they train and perform, gymnasts rub their hands and feet on apparatuses such as the bars and the beam. The friction that results when gymnasts come in contact with apparatuses and mats causes heat and irritates the skin. That can create blisters that may eventually rip open. These are commonly known as "rips." After repeating movements over and over, gymnasts can also develop a callus, or thick layer of protective skin, on areas of their hands and feet. Calluses can only provide limited protection. As gymnasts continue their intense training, friction causes calluses to tear off too.

The best treatment for a ripped blister or callus starts before the rip happens. To prevent rips, gymnasts use lotion on their hands and feet to keep the skin moist. They also try to stop too much of a callus from building up. They soak their hands in water and rub off the callused area with a pumice stone.

When a callus or blister does rip, gymnasts have to make sure all of the loose skin is removed so the skin does not harden and press painfully into the open wound. They either pull the skin off or cut it with sterile scissors. Then, they wash the area and use antibacterial ointment to prevent an infection. Finally, they tape it up with a sterile bandage. Failure to care for these injuries properly can cause bigger problems.

## UNDER THE SKIN

Bruises are also a common injury for gymnasts, who deal often with hard surfaces and wooden equipment. When they make a mistake, they might be knocked into an apparatus or onto the floor. How much force they land with depends on several

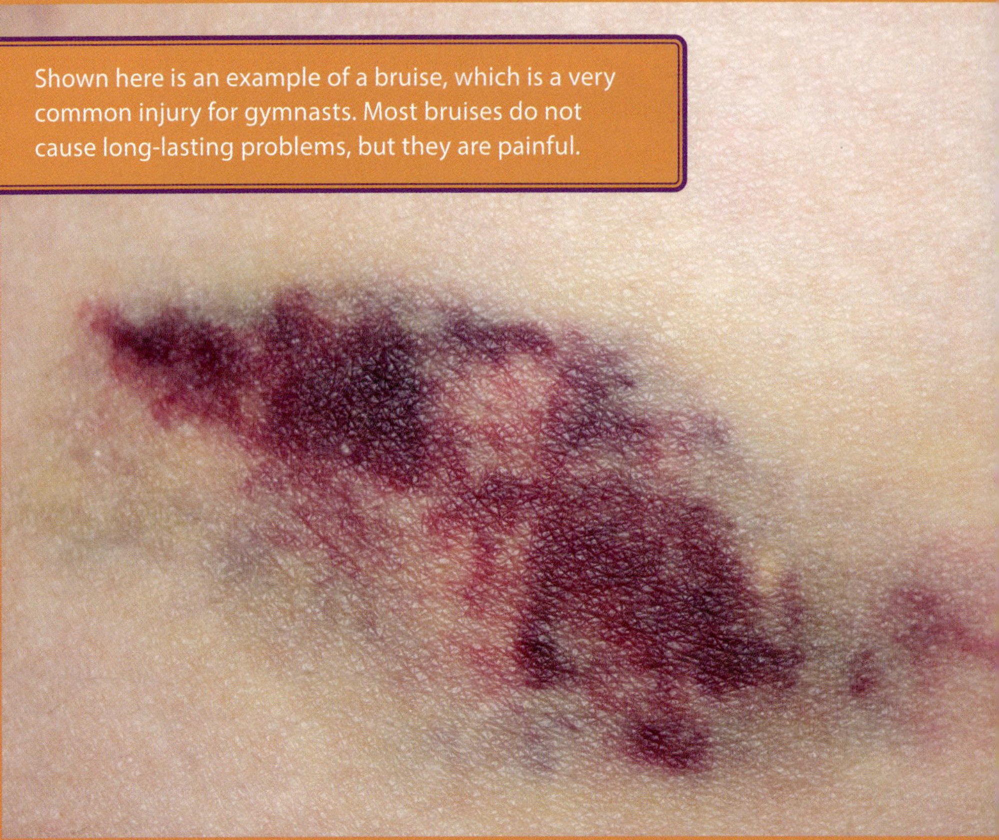

Shown here is an example of a bruise, which is a very common injury for gymnasts. Most bruises do not cause long-lasting problems, but they are painful.

different factors. Velocity can affect the force of impact. A gymnast running toward the vault at a high velocity will crash with more impact than a gymnast running slower.

Falling from a height also presents conditions that can alter the force of impact. Gymnasts will fall faster if they are spinning in a tuck rather than stretched out parallel to the ground. In a tuck, they have less surface area to be slowed by air resistance. In other words, they have lower inertia and a higher angular velocity in a tuck.

In many cases, the impact of a fall causes a bruise, or a contusion, to form on the gymnast's body. A bruise forms when the skin does not break but tiny blood vessels called capillaries rupture, or break, under the skin. The blood from the broken capillaries is trapped under the skin, forming the red and purple marks we know as bruises. They are often very sore and tender when touched, but in most cases, the pain can be lessened with ice. A bruise that doesn't show signs of healing may need extra treatment.

## PERSISTANCE THROUGH PAIN

Most minor injuries caused by gymnastics are not debilitating. They don't need much care, and they do not typically have long-lasting effects. They still hurt, however. Beginners may feel discouraged or frustrated by these minor injuries and the pain that comes with them.

Gymnasts who want to compete at the elite level realize dealing with pain is a part of the sport. They keep training through the aches and pains that come with intense workouts, but sometimes they keep performing even when the injury is more serious. Japanese gymnast Shun Fujimoto is famous for helping his team earn a gold medal at the 1976 Olympic Games by competing with a broken kneecap. After breaking his right kneecap during the floor exercise, he went on to compete on the pommel horse and rings, which made the injury worse. The injury was extremely painful and ended his career as a gymnast. He later said that if he had it to do over again, he would not continue competing while injured.

It is important for gymnasts to learn the difference between everyday soreness and a problematic injury, and it is also important for them to be honest with their coaches about things that are bothering them physically—no matter how small those things may seem. As former Olympic champion Nastia Liukin stated:

> *I've dealt with aches and pains and you certainly put them out of your mind during competition if they're not severe but it's so important to communicate to your coaches, your parents, and your medical staff … If it's spotted early it can be taken care of. If it's really bad, you don't want to make it worse.*[26]

Gymnasts often continue to compete and train while in pain, but they sometimes need to take a break to recover when that

**TWIST AND TURN** In 2023, U.S. gymnast Brody Malone badly injured his knee. After multiple surgeries and much rehab, he came back to win his third U.S. all-around title.

pain comes from something more serious than sore muscles or a rip on their hand. Knowing when to make this call is an important trait for elite gymnasts.

## BODIES AT RISK

All gymnasts compete knowing their sport can cause injuries, sometimes even very serious ones. Many major injuries can be avoided, however, when gymnasts take the proper preventative measures. Warming up and stretching prepare muscles to handle the physical activity to come. Focusing carefully on technique is also essential. When gymnasts pay attention to messages from their proprioceptors, they are less likely to make mistakes that can lead to injuries.

As gymnasts advance in the sport, they perform increasingly dangerous skills. More difficult moves require more speed, height, and flexibility, putting them at greater physical risk. Although elite gymnasts strive for perfection, injuries are always possible, even—and perhaps especially—for the best athletes.

In order to reach and compete at the highest level, elite gymnasts have been known to overwork their bodies. Many have sustained stress fractures as a result. A stress fracture is a break in the bone that results from the physical fatigue that accompanies repetitive motion and impact. Kelly Garrison, who competed for the United States at the 1988 Olympic Games, sustained 22 stress fractures in her spine throughout her career.

Elite gymnasts also typically undergo surgeries throughout their career to repair a variety of major injuries, such as torn muscles and tendons, as well as badly broken bones. When 2004 Olympic all-around gold medalist Paul Hamm fractured his hand in 2008 falling off the parallel bars, he needed surgery to insert a metal plate and nine screws to secure the bone.

## DEALING WITH THE TWISTIES

At the 2020 Summer Olympics (which took place in 2021 because of the COVID-19 pandemic), many eyes were on U.S. star gymnast Simone Biles and the rest of the team. However, the world was stunned when Biles dropped out of the women's artistic team all-around final (and then other events), citing the "twisties" and her mental health.

What are the twisties? According to the Cleveland Clinic, they're a mental block that creates a disconnect between body and mind while a gymnast is airborne. The gymnast loses the all-important sense of where their body is in space: their proprioception sense. This sense isn't only important to gymnasts (it's also key for martial artists and other athletes), but it's particularly dangerous for a gymnast to have this issue. While they're spinning and twisting through the air, losing track of how their body is moving can cause a very nasty fall or bad landing.

Gymnasts with the twisties may take a break to focus on their mental health and go back to some basics for training, building up their skills again to improve their confidence. Simone Biles returned during the Games in 2021 to compete on the balance beam, but then she took an extended break. She made a triumphant Olympic return in 2024, earning four medals (three of them gold), bringing her total to 11 Olympic medals and cementing her status as one of the greatest gymnasts of all time.

The plate and screws held the bone in place so that it could heal properly.

Some gymnasts have paid an even higher price in their quest for success in the sport. In 2012, a 15-year-old upper-level gymnast in Washington State was paralyzed from the chest down after falling on a dismount in practice. In 2006, top Welsh trampoline gymnast Chris Fordham died after falling from a trampoline during practice. He miscalculated his dismount and hit the floor, fracturing his skull on impact. Accidents like this are rare, but they're a sobering reminder that gymnastics can be a dangerous sport.

## A PAUSE TO HEAL

It's not uncommon for gymnasts to be tempted to keep training and competing even while injured. In the end, however, that can worsen the original injury or lead to a secondary injury, which means the first injury causes another. An injured hip, for example, could interfere with the biomechanics of how a gymnast moves. As a result, the gymnast could eventually develop a back injury because their body is trying to compensate for the original injury.

Kerri Strug pulled a stomach muscle when she was training to compete in Europe before the 1996 Olympic Games. She tried to ignore the pain and continue working out, even though the pain got worse each day. She even ignored the advice of a doctor who recommended that she take time off to heal. During the competition in Europe, she injured herself again, and this time it was a more serious injury—a muscle tear.

A major injury such as Strug's would sideline even the most determined athlete. Strug was horrified when doctors told her she would have to wait six months before competing again

Paul Hamm is just one of many gymnasts who have retired to protect their body from further damage.

## BY THE NUMBERS

After the 2024 Olympics, Simone Biles became tied with Věra Čáslavská (1942–2016) for the second-most medals won in women's gymnastics at the Olympics Games. They both have 11, but who's won the most? That honor goes to Larisa Latynina (b. 1934), who won 18 medals in gymnastics for the Soviet Union between 1956 and 1964. Nine of them are gold.

In men's gymnastics, Nikolai Andrianov (1952–2011) of the Soviet Union holds the record with 15 medals, seven of them gold. Of the United States' male gymnasts, Anton Heida (1878–unknown) and George Eyser (1870–1919) are tied with six each.

Paul Hamm (b. 1982) is generally considered the most successful male U.S. gymnast of the modern era. He has three Olympic medals (one of them gold) and is one of only two Americans to win the all-around gymnastics title at both the Olympics and the World Championships. (The other is Biles.)

after her injury. Other top gymnasts have found themselves in similar predicaments. When Paul Hamm was training for the 2008 Olympics, he was dealing with the pain from his fractured hand, a shoulder injury, and a schedule of nonstop training. He wound up withdrawing from the team.

Hamm eventually left the sport when the physical toll on his body no longer seemed worth the chance at a return to Olympic glory. In 2012, he announced his retirement, citing a shoulder injury as one of the reasons his body could no longer handle the intense training required for Olympic gymnasts. Hamm stated a common thought among gymnasts as they age: They have to make the right decision for their body, and often that decision is to leave the sport at a relatively young age before they can damage their body further. "I do have to worry about my body," Hamm said when he announced his retirement. "This is the body I have to carry with me the rest of my life, and hopefully it'll be useful."[27]

Laurie Hernandez proved that it is possible to come back from a serious injury.

## COMEBACKS

Returning to competition in gymnastics after an injury is tough. In most cases, a serious injury requires gymnasts to rest and take time off from physical activity. That enhances the healing process, but elite gymnasts struggle to take time away from the gym. Without regular workouts, they might lose muscle mass and flexibility. In some cases, gymnasts find ways to work out other areas of their body without damaging their injured body part.

Once a gymnast heals, physical therapy helps them regain muscle mass, flexibility, and technical skills. Physical therapy for gymnasts typically involves strength training exercises. Gymnasts may do simple exercises such as lunges and push-ups to build muscle. They might also add weights to create more resistance and build more muscle.

Sometimes, electrical stimulation is used on damaged tissue. When electrical stimulation is used, electrodes are placed on the gymnast's body. An electrical current stimulates the muscle to contract, which helps it grow. The stimulation also improves blood flow to the area.

**TWIST AND TURN** Studies have shown that more than 60 percent of children and teens struggle with body image on a regular basis.

It takes time and patience for a gymnast to make a full recovery. Returning to gymnastics can feel like starting over as a beginner, even for an athlete who formerly competed at the highest level. Laurie Hernandez, a member of 2016's Final Five, suffered multiple knee injuries in the years before making her Olympic debut, but she credited her support system with helping her recover and receive the treatment she needed:

> *If we have to go out of our way to make a doctor's appointment or if I need someone to take me to therapy, someone's always there to help. Even all the gym moms and dads are always helping to get me to the gym or to even help with taking me to doctors' appointments.*[28]

Coming back from an injury is not easy, but with proper medical treatment, the right amount of rest, and a sense of competitive drive, gymnasts can bounce back. Many gymnasts have said that coming back from an injury has made them more motivated. Some are able to rise to greater heights than even before their injury.

## UNDER PRESSURE

Recovering from an injury is just one of many things that can increase the pressure that gymnasts are under to succeed. When gymnasts are working toward a particular competition, they cannot afford to lose training time. Even when a competition is not approaching immediately, the pressure is particularly intense for female gymnasts throughout their gymnastics career. Female gymnasts' bodies change dramatically with the onset of puberty. Once they develop hips and breasts, their bodies are not as light and streamlined as they were before puberty. This has made many female gymnasts self-conscious about their bodies and has led to disordered eating habits among many female gymnasts who hoped to combat the effects of puberty by remaining as thin as possible.

As puberty approaches, female gymnasts experience psychological changes as well. Young girls often lose confidence when their bodies change. That puts them at risk when unethical coaches use their feelings against them. "Studies show that a young girl's self-esteem plummets much more dramatically than that of a boy at a similar stage in life," reporter Joan Ryan wrote. "Self-conscious about her looks and sensitive about her body, in particular her weight, she is a mass of insecurities looking for an identity."[29] This can lead to abuse by authority figures who aren't trustworthy.

## ISSUES OF PHYSICAL AND PSYCHOLOGICAL ABUSE

A gymnast's intense training often involves a strict schedule. They may spend many hours in the gym each day. Some coaches use that busy schedule to gain control of their gymnasts' minds. They might isolate their gymnasts from family and friends. Some tell their gymnasts that they are fat and demand

McKayla Maroney was one of the gymnasts who spoke about being abused by Larry Nassar.

**TWIST AND TURN** Four female gymnasts have made the U.S. Olympic team three times in a row: Simone Biles (2016, 2020, 2024), Dominique Dawes (1992, 1996, 2000), Linda Metheny (1964, 1968, 1972), and Muriel Grossfeld (1956, 1960, 1964).

that they lose weight, even when they are actually underweight for their height. There are also coaches who use a variety of bullying tactics, such as verbal abuse, swearing, and physical violence, to control athletes.

Gymnasts have also reported sexual abuse. In December 2016, *IndyStar* released a comprehensive report covering 20 years of abuse allegations, and it was discovered that at least 368 gymnasts reported some form of sexual abuse during those two decades. The abuse came at the hands of people entrusted with their development and care, including coaches and gym owners. Then, in January 2017, 18 women and girls filed a lawsuit against Larry Nassar, a former USA Gymnastics doctor who sexually assaulted them during physical exams. Nassar was later convicted on multiple federal and state charges against hundreds of victims. Many of those he abused had reported the abuse before.

Psychological abuse can be just as damaging to gymnasts as physical and sexual abuse. When gymnasts are verbally abused or fear physical or sexual abuse, they may feel nervous, afraid, and upset. They may lose their ability to trust their own judgment or stop listening to other people who care about them. Even the most focused athletes may begin to abuse themselves as a result. That can lead to more physical and psychological problems.

Some gymnasts push their body too hard after an injury or starve themselves to try to achieve what their coaches tell them is the ideal body of a gymnast. Dominique Moceanu, who was part of the 1996 U.S. Olympic team, wrote in her memoirs about the psychological trauma she experienced under the Karolyis. Moceanu stated that their damaging mind games made gymnasts push

## CARING FOR MENTAL HEALTH

Gymnasts are under a lot of pressure, and one way they can deal with it is by seeing a mental health professional, such as a sports psychologist. A sports psychologist can help gymnasts gain confidence in their own ability, reduce their anxiety, view their body in a more positive way, and handle the stress they are under in healthy ways.

Simone Biles has used a sports psychologist to help her reach her full potential. Sports psychologist, Robert Andrews, who has worked with Biles, stated that her team's openness when it comes to addressing mental blocks and confidence issues is refreshing. "It's remarkable they've been so vocal about it," he has said. "Most athletes, particularly male athletes, wouldn't dare talk about seeing someone in my field. I hope they open the door to our field being more recognized and supported, because it is vital."[1]

1. Quoted in Alyssa Roenigk, "Meet the Coach Who Helps Simone Biles, Laurie Hernandez Stay MentallyStrong," ESPNW, August 9, 2016. www.espn.com/espnw/sports/article/17252340/mental-gymnasticsmeet-sports-psychology-coach-keeps-simone-biles-laurie-hernandez-sharp.

themselves even when they were dealing with serious injuries and intense pain:

> *If I had ever started to talk about my pain or injury, they would immediately cut me off, dismissing it or making comments or gestures that I was becoming weak, faking, or exaggerating injury out of laziness.*
>
> *These negative mind games were a regular part of their coaching style and confused my psyche. I actually started to buy in to their psychology and believe that, perhaps, I didn't hurt* that *much and the sharp drilling pain in my leg was coming from my head. I remember thinking,* Is it my fault that I am in so much pain?[30]

Moceanu also stated that the Karolyis used to tell her that she needed to lose weight, although she was severely underweight for her height and age. Comments about female

Gymnasts are often under a lot of stress. It is important for them to talk to someone about it.

gymnasts' weight are common and can have fatal consequences. Gymnast Christy Henrich took it to heart when a judge told her in 1988 that she needed to lose weight to make it to the Olympics. Henrich then expressed concerns to her coach that she was not thin enough to compete in the sport. She kept losing weight and strength and soon retired from gymnastics altogether. Henrich suffered from anorexia nervosa, which is characterized by starvation, and bulimia nervosa, which is characterized by bingeing and purging. Both are serious eating disorders. Her condition spiraled out of control. She eventually died, in 1994, of multiple organ failure resulting from her weight loss. It was a wake-up call to some, but these issues persist.

## HEALTHY BODY AND MIND

Many top gymnasts find ways to manage the mental pressures of intense training, including seeing sports psychologists and other mental health professionals. Some gymnasts are able to make a connection with their coaches, so they do not get upset at constructive criticism. Not all gymnastics coaches believe abusive tactics and total control are the best means to create champions. Most understand gymnasts need support from friends and family as well as freedom to determine the direction of their own lives. Gymnastics coach Liang Chow, for example, did not allow Olympic gymnast Shawn Johnson to train too hard. Her training schedule allowed time for her to attend public school and have a social life. Chow's approach also helped Johnson escape major injuries because she did not train too intensely. "With a loving environment, everyone can do more,"[31] he told *USA Today*.

Other gymnasts use their own techniques to keep control of their training schedules, their bodies, and their lives. Rest days are very important for both gymnasts' physical health and mental health. Both Gabby Douglas and Aly Raisman said that they took one day off each week to rest their body and focus on things other than the pressure that comes with their sport. As Douglas said, "One of the things I love to do on my days off is *not* talk about gymnastics."[32]

Many gymnasts relax by doing things such as getting massages, watching movies, and taking baths. These things may seem like simple luxuries, but as Raisman said, "I think resting, relaxation, and clearing your mind is one of the healthiest things you can do."[33] This is why some gymnasts also practice meditation, which has been scientifically proven to help people focus and reduce their anxiety.

When coaches—and the gymnasts themselves—are mindful of gymnasts' mental health, the psychological effects of the sport are positive. Learning new moves teaches gymnasts perseverance and develops concentration skills. Gymnasts also build self-control and discipline. When they master new skills, they gain self-esteem.

It's important for athletes, no matter their level, to be healthy in body and mind. Many gymnasts, including Simone Biles, have begun speaking more openly about their mental health. This is sure to inspire future gymnasts to see mental health as an important factor in their overall health and success in the sport.

# CHAPTER SIX

# MOVING FORWARD

The roots of gymnastics go back a very long time, further than most other major sports. This long history doesn't mean that it is stuck in the past, however. Technological advances have made and continue to make the sport better and safer.

The development of safer equipment is one example of technology being used to improve the sport. The change from the horse to the vaulting table in 2001 was completed after engineers worked to develop the safest apparatus possible. The balance beam has also changed over time to become safer for gymnasts. What was once simply a wooden beam is now covered with leather to increase the friction between the apparatus and a gymnast's hands and feet. This has decreased the likelihood of a gymnast slipping off the beam, because the wooden surface was more slippery.

Technological advances have also changed the ways gymnasts recover from injuries and take care of their bodies after training. New fabrics for leotards are more aerodynamic. Technology is also being studied and tested to make scoring in gymnastics more objective and precise. In many ways, the eyes of the gymnastics world are on the future.

## BE CHILL

Gymnasts often use ice as a common treatment for injuries and soreness. Some use baths in ice water to recover from intense training sessions. Today, though, some athletes take the idea of treating their body with cold temperatures to the extreme. Gymnasts have joined the ranks of athletes from many other sports, including baseball, football, and basketball, who use a treatment called cryotherapy to help their body recover from the strain their sport puts on it.

Cryotherapy involves putting the body in a chamber that is blasted with liquid nitrogen, which creates very cold temperatures. In fact, temperatures in a cryotherapy chamber can reach as low as −300 degrees Fahrenheit (−184.4 degrees Celsius). A gymnast remains in the chamber for two to

Cryotherapy has become a popular wellness trend, but experts caution that it is not a cure-all.

## QUESTIONS ON CRYOTHERAPY

Athletes may use cryotherapy to help their muscles recover, but others claim that it can help with many other medical conditions. Some say cryotherapy can be used to treat people who suffer from arthritis, chronic pain, and depression, among other diseases and disorders.

The FDA, however, cited in a report that there is more solid proof of the dangers of the treatment than the benefits of it. As of early 2025, it hasn't approved the treatment. A scientific reviewer for the FDA stated:

> *Potential hazards include asphyxiation, especially when liquid nitrogen is used for cooling … The addition of nitrogen vapors to a closed room lowers the amount of oxygen in the room and can result in hypoxia, or oxygen deficiency, which could lead the user to lose consciousness. Moreover, subjects run the risk of frostbite, burns, and eye injury from the extreme temperatures.*[1]

1. Quoted in "Whole Body Cryotherapy (WBC): A 'Cool' Trend that Lacks Evidence, Poses Risks," U.S. Food and Drug Administration, July 5, 2016. www.fda.gov/ForConsumers/ConsumerUpdates/ucm508739.htm.

three minutes. During this time, their body goes into survival mode, and the blood rushes to protect the vital organs. Then, when the gymnast gets out of the chamber, the blood rushes to the rest of the body, helping their muscles recover.

The International Olympic Committee (IOC) has included cryotherapy on its lists of approved recovery methods for Olympic athletes, and gymnasts have posted about their cryotherapy treatments on social media. However, the U.S. Food and Drug Administration (FDA) has issued a warning against cryotherapy, stating that there is no clear evidence that it is an effective medical treatment. "Given a growing interest from consumers in whole body cryotherapy, the FDA has informally reviewed the medical literature available on this subject," a medical officer for the FDA stated. "We found very little evidence about its safety or effectiveness in treating the conditions for which it is being promoted."[34] Despite the lack of medical evidence supporting cryotherapy, some people still swear by it.

# COMPRESSION DEVICES

While some gymnasts believe that cryotherapy is the key to recovery after training and competing, others prefer compression. Simone Biles is just one of the elite gymnasts who can sometimes be seen on social media wearing something that looks like a thick pair of pants, which is actually an air compression system designed to improve recovery time.

Compression devices are placed on specific parts of the body, such as the legs, arms, or hips, and inflate, or fill with air. That air is then used to compress and release the muscles in a pulsing pattern. This acts as a kind of massage, increasing the movement of fluid in the body after a workout and enhancing circulation. Gymnasts believe that it helps reduce soreness and keeps their muscles in the best shape possible so they can continue to train and compete at a high level.

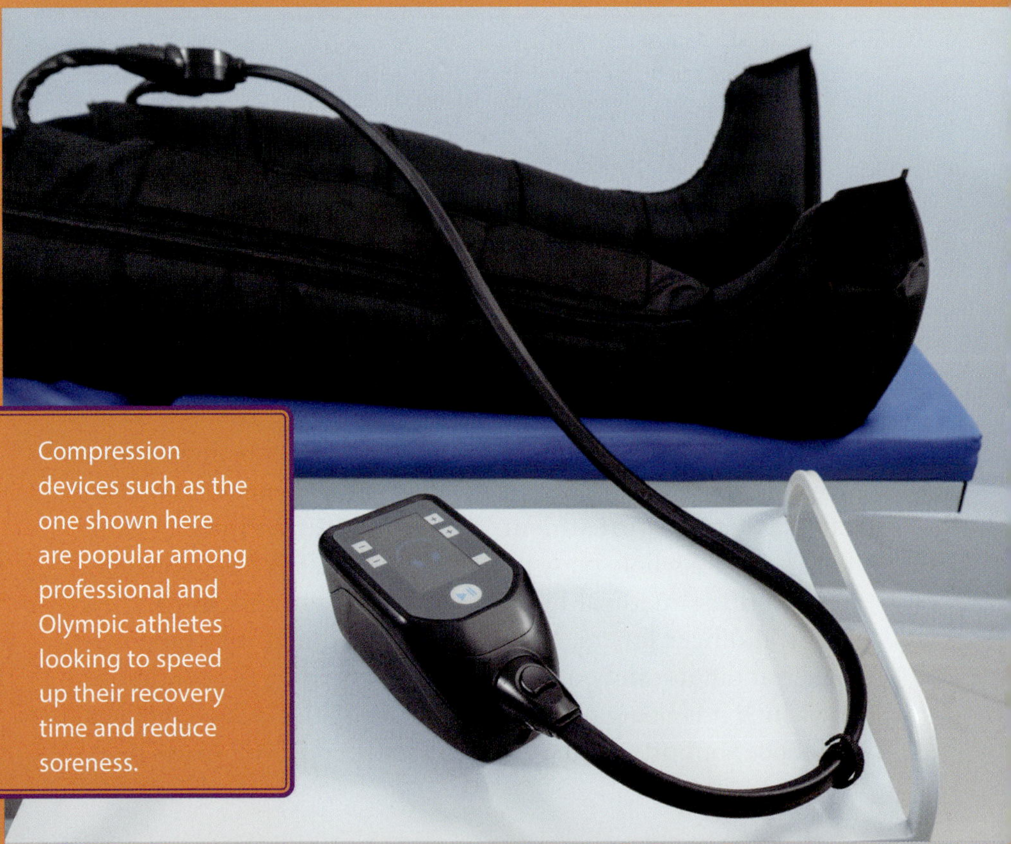

Compression devices such as the one shown here are popular among professional and Olympic athletes looking to speed up their recovery time and reduce soreness.

**TWIST AND TURN** Lactic acid is produced in muscles during exercise when oxygen levels are low and glucose is broken down. This contributes to soreness after a workout.

Although there is not much scientific research on the benefits of compression devices and much of the research that has been conducted to date is inconclusive, some scientific and medical journals have endorsed the use of this treatment method. For example, the *Journal of Strength and Conditioning Research* has that dynamic compression "is a promising means of accelerating and enhancing recovery after the normal aggressive training that occurs in Olympic and aspiring Olympic athletes."[35]

## AI AND SCORING

Another relatively new and interesting way in which technology is being applied to gymnastics is in the area of judging and scoring. Changes to the scoring system have aimed to make the sport as objective as possible, but when humans judge a sport, human error is, of course, always possible. For example, the human eye cannot catch every angle of every limb during a gymnastics routine, so judges naturally miss things that could have affected the scoring.

In 2019, the International Gymnastics Federation first used the Judging Support System (JSS) developed by the Japanese company Fujitsu to help judge several events at the World Championships. Since then, it has been expanded to all apparatuses in competition. This artificial intelligence (AI) technology uses high-definition cameras to capture a 3D view when a gymnast is performing. The AI model is trained on the gymnastics Code of Points, an extensive guide to just about every element a gymnast could perform. It can identify about 2,000 elements.

Previously, gymnasts would have needed to place motion capture sensors all over their body to provide judges with such a clear and precise analysis of their technique. However, motion capture technology is not practical because the sensors interfere with a gymnast's movements. At first, scientists were going to use lasers with the AI technology, but the system as used now is based entirely on cameras.

The scientists who originated the technology also see applications for other sports. In an official press release, Fujitsu Laboratories stated:

> *In addition to reducing the burden on judges in the face of increasingly complex and sophisticated gymnastics techniques, it is also expected to reduce the time required for scoring in competitions, benefitting both athletes and spectators. This technology, when applied for viewing and training, is anticipated to be useful beyond gymnastics and other judging system-based competitions.*[36]

There are other possible gymnastics uses for this technology as well. Athletes and coaches may also be able to use it to analyze performances in practice to improve technique and avoid injury. Broadcasters may even be able to use it to explain the fine points of a performance to viewers at home.

## SUCCESS THROUGH SCIENCE

The sport of gymnastics has always been about scientific forces at its core, and gymnasts and those who train and judge them are always looking for new ways to understand these forces better to keep their sport moving forward. These forces include the friction that keeps gymnasts from falling and the gravity that keeps them from soaring into the stratosphere. With a better understanding of these principles comes a better understanding of how gymnasts can improve their technique, their height on jumps and flips, and their chances for executing even the most challenging moves safely.

Understanding science can be a key to understanding gymnastics in a more in-depth and even more entertaining way. If you know a bit about physics, you can better admire how a gymnast uses the perfect amount of force to push off the ground and execute an incredible move. If you have a good grasp of biology, you can understand just how difficult some gymnastics feats are in terms of how they push, stretch, and challenge the human body. And if you understand the engineering behind new technologies, you can better appreciate how they can make the sport even more amazing to watch!

Knowing the science behind gymnastics makes the sport even more impressive to watch!

# NOTES

## Chapter One: Art and Science


1. Chloe Angyai, "Here's The Real Reason We Love Watching Olympic Gymnastics," *The Huffington Post*, August 12, 2016. www.huffingtonpost.com/entry/the-real-reason-we-love-watching-olympic-gymnastics_us_57a4e794e4b021fd98789d06.

2. Reeves Wiedeman, "A Full Revolution," *The New Yorker*, May 30, 2016. www.newyorker.com/magazine/2016/05/30/simone-biles-is-the-best-gymnast-in-the-world.

3. Quoted in Nancy Armour, "40 Years After Perfect 10, Gymnast Nadia Comaneci Remains an Olympic Icon," *USA Today*, July 20, 2016. www.usatoday.com/story/sports/olympics/rio-2016/2016/07/20/10-gymnast-nadia-comaneci-olympics-montreal/87357146/.

4. Nadia Comăneci, *Letters to a Young Gymnast*, New York, NY: Basic Books, 2004, p. 23.

5. Quoted in Mike Reilley, "It's Dangerous From the Start: Gymnastics: Some Officials and Coaches Wonder if the Spectacular Yurchenko Vault is Worth the Risk," *Los Angeles Times*, November 17, 1989. articles.latimes.com/1989-11-17/sports/sp-1670_1_yurchenko-vault.

6. Quoted in Liz Clarke, "For Olympic Gymnasts, It's Usually One and Done," *The Washington Post*, November 9, 2012. www.washingtonpost.com/sports/olympics/for-olympic-gymnasts-its-usually-one-and-done/2012/11/09/c3dc8788-2ab9-11e2-96b6-8e6a7524553f_story.html?utm_term=.35bb3ba768c7.

7. Quoted in Rachel Axon, "Raisman Quietly Builds One of USA's Best Olympics Gymnastics Records," *USA Today*, August 15, 2016. www.usatoday.com/story/sports/olympics/rio-2016/2016/08/15/gymnastics-aly-raisman-gold-medal-usa/88795986/.

8. Juliet Macur, "Gymnast's Specialty: Returning to the Olympics. (She's 41. It's Her 7th Trip.)," *New York Times*, August 14, 2016. www.nytimes.com/2016/08/15/sports/olympics/oksana-chusovitina-gymnastics-rio-games.html.

9. Juliet Macur, "A 10 Isn't Necessarily Perfect in New Scoring System for Gymnastics," *New York Times*, August 5, 2008. www.nytimes.com/2008/08/06/sports/olympics/06scoring.html.

10. Bill Chappel, "U.S. Women's Gymnastics Team Wins Gold Medal: Live Blog," NPR, August 9, 2016. www.npr.org/sections/thetorch/2016/08/09/489352987/live-blog-u-s-women-s-gymnastics-team-goes-for-gold.

## Chapter Two: Balance Basics

11. Quoted in Jon Hamilton, "How a 'Sixth Sense' Helps Simone Biles Fly, and the Rest of Us Walk," NPR, September 21, 2016. www.npr.org/sections/health-shots/2016/09/21/494887467/how-a-sixth-sense-helps-simone-biles-fly-and-the-rest-of-us-walk.

## Chapter Three: Flying High

12. Mary Lou Retton and Bela Karolyi with John Powers, *Mary Lou: Creating an Olympic Champion*. New York, NY: McGraw-Hill, 1986, p. 11.

13. Sarah Sloat, "Why Simone Biles Won't Attempt the 'Vault of Death,'" *The Huffington Post*, August 19, 2016. www.huffingtonpost.com/inverse/why-simone-biles-wont-att_b_11610642.html.

14. Kurt Thomas and Kent Hannon, *Kurt Thomas on Gymnastics*. New York, NY: Simon & Schuster, 1980, p. 37.

15. Comăneci, *Letters to a Young Gymnast*, p. 151.

16. Retton and Karolyi, *Mary Lou*, p. 20.

## Chapter Four: Training Trials

17. Quoted in Alice Park, "Making Gymnastics Safer for Kids," *TIME*, April 8, 2008. www.time.com/time/health/article/0,8599,1728902,00.html.

18. Quoted in Liz Clarke, "Meet Simone Biles, Who Is About to Turn Olympic Gymnastics Upside Down," *The Washington Post*, July 1, 2016. www.washingtonpost.com/news/sports/wp/2016/07/01/meet-simone-biles-who-is-about-to-turn-olympic-gymnastics-upside-down/?utm_term=.c2e2b2be905a.

19. Quoted in Elizabeth Narins, "What a World Class Olympian Really Eats," *Cosmopolitan*, May 31, 2016. www.cosmopolitan.com/health-fitness/a58597/aly-raisman-diet-diary/.

20. Clarke, "For Olympic Gymnasts, It's Usually One and Done."

21. Julie Mazziotta, "Shawn Johnson Opens Up About Her Eating Disorder: 'I Would Eat 700 Calories a Day,'" *People*, November 23, 2015. people.com/sports/shawn-johnson-talks-about-eating-disorder-would-eat-700-calories-a-day/.

22. Quoted in Mazziotta, "Shawn Johnson Opens Up About Her Eating Disorder."

23. Quoted in Rose Minutaglio, "Simone Biles on Overcoming Body-Shaming from Coach: 'It Just Taught Me to Rise Above,'" *People*, November 16, 2016. people.com/sports/simone-biles-on-overcoming-body-shaming-from-coach-it-just-taught-me-to-rise-above/.

24. Quoted in Minutaglio, "Simone Biles on Overcoming Body-Shaming from Coach."

## Chapter Five: Science of Safety

25. Quoted in Park, "Making Gymnastics Safer for Kids."

26. Quoted in Liz Neporent, "Olympic Gymnast Injuries: Does Working Through Pain Send Wrong Message to Kids?," ABC News, September 12, 2012. abcnews.go.com/Health/olympic-gymnast-injuries-wrong-message-kids/story?id=17216974.

27. Quoted in "Olympic Gymnast Paul Hamm Retires, Says Body Can't Handle Training," *Sports Illustrated*, March 27, 2012. www.si.com/more-sports/2012/03/27/paul-hamm-retires.

28. Quoted in Steve Lichtenstein, "Jersey Teen Laurie Hernandez Undeterred in Mission for Olympic Gold," CBS New York, July 18, 2016. newyork.cbslocal.com/2016/07/18/laurie-hernandez-team-usa-olympics-gymnast/.

29. Joan Ryan, *Little Girls in Pretty Boxes: The Making and Breaking of Elite Gymnasts and Figure Skaters*. New York, NY: Doubleday, 1995, p. 205.

30. Quoted in Jessica Winter, "The Karolyis' Tainted Glory," *Slate*, August 12, 2016. www.slate.com/articles/sports/fivering_circus/2016/08/martha_karolyi_and_her_husband_bela_were_great_coaches_they_also_allegedly.html.

31. Quoted in Marlen Garcia, "Shawn Johnson's Roots Run from Iowa to Beijing," *USA Today*, August 6, 2008. www.usatoday.com/sports/olympics/beijing/gymnastics/2008-08-06-johnson_N.htm.

32. Quoted in Elizabeth Narins, "What Olympic Gymnast Gabby Douglas Really Eats in a Day," *Cosmopolitan*, July 13, 2016. www.cosmopolitan.com/health-fitness/news/a60797/what-olympic-gymnast-gabby-douglas-really-eats-in-a-day/.

33. Quoted in Narins, "What a World Class Olympian Really Eats."

## Chapter Six: Moving Forward

34. Quoted in "Whole Body Cryotherapy (WBC): A 'Cool' Trend that Lacks Evidence, Poses Risks," U.S. Food and Drug Administration, July 5, 2016. www.fda.gov/ForConsumers/ConsumerUpdates/ucm508739.htm.

35. Quoted in W.A. Sands, J. R. McNeal, S. R. Murray, and M. H. Stone, "Dynamic Compression Enhances Pressure-to-Pain Threshold in Elite Athlete Recovery: Exploratory Study," PubMed.gov, May 2015. www.ncbi.nlm.nih.gov/pubmed/24531439.

36. Japan Gymnastics Association, Fujitsu Limited, Fujitsu Laboratories Ltd., "Japan Gymnastics Association and Fujitsu Agree to Jointly Research Scoring Support Technology for Competitions," Fujitsu, May 17, 2016. www.fujitsu.com/global/about/resources/news/press-releases/2016/0517-02.html#1.

# GLOSSARY

**aerodynamic**: Able to easily move through air.
**agile**: Characterized by quick, graceful movements.
**apparatus**: Equipment designed for a specific use.
**cardiovascular system**: The system in the human body made up of the heart and blood vessels.
**cerebellum**: The part of the brain that controls coordination and equilibrium.
**dynamic stretching**: Active movements of the muscles that involve stretching without holding the body in the stretch's end position.
**fracture**: A break, especially in a bone.
**gravity**: A force of attraction between two objects in the universe.
**kinetic energy**: Energy of motion.
**ligament**: A tough band of tissue that connects bones or supports an organ in its place in the body.
**mass**: The amount of matter contained in an object.
**metabolize**: To change food into a substance that can be used by the body.
**momentum**: A property of a moving body that depends on its mass and velocity.
**puberty**: The age or period of time in which the body of a boy or girl matures and becomes capable of reproducing.
**respiratory system**: The group of body parts that play a role in breathing.
**sterile**: Completely clean and free from all bacteria and other microorganisms.
**weight**: A measurement of gravity's force on an object.

# FOR MORE INFORMATION

## BOOKS

Biles, Simone, Michelle Buford, and Mary Lou Retton. *Courage to Soar: A Body in Motion, A Life in Balance*. Grand Rapids, MI: Zondervan, 2016.

Goldstein, Margaret J. *Epic Gymnastics Moments*. Minneapolis, MN: Lerner Publications, 2024.

Harris, Beatrice. *STEM in Gymnastics*. Buffalo, NY: Cavendish Square Publishing, 2025.

Joyce, Andrea. *Legends of Women's Gymnastics*. New York, NY: Abbeville Kids, 2024.

Lawrence, Blythe. *Trailblazing Women in Gymnastics*. Chicago, IL: Norwood House Press, 2023.

Monnig, Alex. *Gymnastics*. Minneapolis, MN: A & D Xtreme, 2023.

## WEBSITES

**FIG Channel: YouTube**
***www.youtube.com/user/figchannel***
The official FIG YouTube channel has videos that explain different gymnastics disciplines and showcase competition highlights, giving viewers a look at gymnastics in action at the highest level.

**The Fine Line: Simone Biles Gymnastics**
***www.nytimes.com/interactive/2016/08/05/sports/olympics-gymnast-simone-biles.html***
This interactive *New York Times* feature takes a closer look at how Simone Biles pulls off the impressive gymnastic feats she has become famous for.

**Safety Tips for Gymnastics**
***kidshealth.org/en/teens/safety-gymnastics.html#***
This website presents valuable information about how to stay safe and healthy if you are interested in becoming a gymnast.

**Science of Sport: Gymnastics**
***www.wired.com/video/2016/08/science-of-sport-gymnastics***
*Wired* magazine produced this short, informative video, in which leading gymnasts, including Aly Raisman, explain some of the scientific concepts at work in gymnastics.

**USA Gymnastics**
***usagym.org***
The official website of USA Gymnastics features information about the sport, competition results, and a tool that allows young people and their parents to find a gymnastics training center in their area.

# INDEX

# PICTURE CREDITS

Cover, Alex Kravtsov/Shutterstock.com; Cover, pp. 1, 3-104 hero mujahid/Shutterstock.com; Cover, pp. 1, 3, 4, 6, 23, 36, 51, 67, 83, 87, 94, 96, 98, 103, 104 marooshka/Shutterstock.com; Cover, pp. 1, 3 - 104 Free Icon Download/Shutterstock.com; pp. 5, 52 ADDICTIVE STOCK/Shutterstock.com; pp. 7, 17, 33, 65 A.RICARDO/Shutterstock.com; p. 9 https://commons.wikimedia.org/wiki/File:Schuhmann_flatow_weingartner.jpg; p. 12 Artur Didyk/Shutterstock.com; p. 15 Science History Images / Alamy Stock Photo; p. 19 Colin McPhedran/Shutterstock.com; p. 21 Leonard Zhukovsky/Shutterstock.com; pp. 24, 40, 47 Alex Bogatyrev/Shutterstock.com; p. 26 PeopleImages.com - Yuri A/Shutterstock.com; p. 28 Rawpixel.com/Shutterstock.com; p. 30 Bukavik/Shutterstock.com; p. 34 Jiang Dao Hua/Shutterstock.com; p. 37 Victor Velter/Shutterstock.com; p. 38 Polhansen/Shutterstock.com; p. 42 Goolia Photography/Shutterstock.com; p. 45 PA Images / Alamy Stock Photo; pp. 49, 63, 74 PCN Photography / Alamy Stock Photo; p. 53 Oleggg/Shutterstock.com; p. 54 Focus Pix/Shutterstock.com; p. 56 WoodysPhotos/Shutterstock.com; p. 59 Anatoliy Karlyuk/Shutterstock.com; p. 68 ChooChin/Shutterstock.com; p. 70 Alexander Sobol/Shutterstock.com; p. 76 Leonard Zhukovsky/Shutterstock.com; p. 78 UPI / Alamy Stock Photo; p. 81 BearFotos/Shutterstock.com; p. 84 Jacob Lund/Shutterstock.com; p. 86 Pictures of your Life/Shutterstock.com; p. 89 Real Sports Photos/Shutterstock.com.

# ABOUT THE AUTHOR

**AMY B. ROGERS** is an experienced nonfiction author who has written many books for young readers on topics that include American history, science, and women's participation in sports. She lives in a suburb of Buffalo, New York, with her husband, Steve, and their Welsh corgi, Jiminy.